THE NEW AGENDA

Achieving Personalized Learning Through Digital Convergence

DR. SHAWN K. SMITH

Todd Stansfield, Editor
Sara Plampin, Copy Editor

MAGNUSSON-SKOR

Denver
www.magnussonskor.com

Published by

Magnusson-Skor Publishing LLC
4600 S. Ulster Street Suite 1050
Denver, CO 80237
www.magnussonskor.com

Library of Congress Cataloging-in-Publication Data

Smith, Shawn K., 1975-
Ed. Todd Stansfield
Copy Ed. Sara Plampin

   The New Agenda: Achieving Personalized Learning Through
   Digital Convergence.
   p. cm.
   Includes biographical references.
   ISBN 978-0-9842051-5-8, 978-0-9842051-6-5
   1. Digital Convergence 2. Personalized Learning 3. Modern Learning
   Environment 4. Twenty-First Century Teaching and Learning I. Title

First Edition

For Today's Modern Leaders

CONTENTS

vi

ACKNOWLEDGEMENTS

I owe special thanks to several notable individuals who were instrumental in the development and publication of this book. I would like to acknowledge the entire team at Modern Teacher for their collective insights, feedback, and vision to replace the traditional classroom with the modern learning environment. Your contributions helped shape and refine the lessons and commentary contained in these pages.

I would also like to thank the Modern Teacher Network—a national network of school districts—for its inspiring and informative efforts to champion the movement toward personalized learning. Its member districts serve as pioneers for other districts to follow.

I would also like to pay special thanks to the National Council on Digital Convergence for its thought leadership around twenty-first century teaching and learning. This collective body brings together today's most innovative minds on transforming education for the modern age. National Council members include Dr. David Richards; Dr. J.R. Proctor; Dr. Peter Gorman; Kevin Case; Dr. Lori Duerr; Ryan Imbriale; Jeanne Imbriale; Dr. Barbara Nesbitt; Charlene Simpson; and Dr. Todd Keruskin.

Additionally, I would like to recognize several key individuals who made significant contributions to the research and discoveries contained in this book. They include Dr. Ann M. Chavez, Garrett Seaman, Jeff Ottens, Lisette Casey, Mike Smith, Laura Janusek, Patti Barrett, Sarah Folzenlogen, and Stephanie Hollar. Thank you for your tireless efforts.

I would also like to thank Todd Stansfield, my editor, whose persistent advice, revisions, coaching, and eye were critical to the success of this project.

Lastly, I would like to acknowledge the ongoing mentorship, support, and direction of Charles L. Fred. Without you, Charles, this book would not have been possible. Thank you.

Preface

Our journey to uncover the concept of Digital Convergence began with a recognition that K–12 education was years behind other industries on the technology adoption continuum. As most industries were embracing technology to transform the consumer experience, K–12 education remained constrained to the analog mindsets, processes, and structures that have existed since the Industrial Revolution. Given the promises afforded by the digital revolution—such as personalized and individualized learning—my colleagues and I sought to uncover the reasons why technology wasn't gaining traction in K–12. More importantly, we sought a method and approach to help our industry move into the modern age.

We began by analyzing how a handful of prominent education leaders were pioneering the transition to modern learning environments—environments that facilitate personalized, blended learning and overcome the deficiencies of the one-size-fits-all approach to education. As we began our quest, we sought to uncover what these education leaders were doing, how they were doing it, what decisions they were making, and how they were managing the change process. So we spent time with them. We watched and chronicled their actions and began synthesizing our findings. We visited over 9,000 classrooms across the country and developed the Digital Convergence Framework—a practical and validated approach for others embarking on the journey to transform teaching and learning for the twenty-first century.

The framework will help guide you in the journey, support your leadership decisions, and offer a strategic lens through which to view this work. It's intended to identify critical questions every leader must inevitably consider. Included in the framework are success indicators, or action items, with which to measure your progress. This methodology involves setting goals within goal cycles and measuring your work against those objectives.

The framework is not, however, intended to give you step-by-step instructions to achieve Digital Convergence. Instead, it's a structure that guides you through a series of important action items in five key areas of work, or drivers, at the school-district level. We've found that great leaders intentionally concentrate on the five drivers in non-linear fashion and constantly inquire how each area of work interrelates. They also form a series of teams and work groups to focus on each driver and carefully implement systems and processes to ensure no single group makes decisions in isolation or advances ahead of another. These leaders also build internal expertise and ensure that internal stakeholders can speak to their vision and journey toward Digital Convergence. In the process, they become a powerful vehicle for change.

Part I of this book introduces you to the challenges facing

our industry—challenges that have slowed our adoption and effective integration of technology. From the accelerating rate of technological change to factors internal to our districts—you gain insight into the barriers of the modern, or personalized, learning environment.

Part II explores the solution to the challenges preventing our districts from transforming teaching and learning for the modern age. In this section, you learn about the concept of Digital Convergence, including its five drivers. These drivers include activities around leadership, instructional models, curriculum, digital resources, and professional learning. I also explain the Digital Convergence Framework and its use.

Part III explores the first three stages of the Digital Convergence Framework, which illustrate the early and emerging progress of districts engaged in this work. Here, I outline the tactical action items needed to make progress in the journey toward Digital Convergence. You learn about each stage in detail across the five drivers of Convergence and gain insight into the specific action items, called success indicators, that demonstrate advancement.

This book does not detail technological solutions or explore the in-depth changes occurring today in K–12 education. Instead, it serves as a practical guide for you, the superintendents and educational leaders of K–12, who, in accepting the need to transform your district through technology, may feel overwhelmed by the number of solutions in the industry today, all of which promise to heal systemic problems with single-point, near-sighted solutions—solutions that ignore the underlying causes of the problem and offer only temporary relief of symptoms. This book offers you a new lens to approach technology integration more thoughtfully, systematically, and fundamentally. It also teaches you to understand systems and change management.

THE
NEW
AGENDA

Achieving Personalized Learning
Through Digital Convergence

INTRODUCTION

This book is for superintendents and educational leaders who feel like they're leading their districts and communities from inside a turbulent, unpredictable storm.

Leaders who are overwhelmed by the accelerated pace of technological change.

Leaders who share the moral imperative to replace the traditional classroom with a modern, or personalized, learning environment.

Leaders who are struggling to produce graduates with skills and competencies to compete on a global scale.

Leaders who are seeking a solution to advance their districts in the face of tumult and uncertainty.

Historically, K–12 education has answered society's call to produce graduates with skills to compete in the industries of the time. As the transition from horsepower to steam power gave rise to the Industrial Age, our school systems adapted, just as they did with the emergence of the internet and arrival of the Information Age. Yet now K–12 education finds itself in uncertain territory. As Thomas Friedman notes in his book *Thank You for Being Late*, the rise of globalization, technological innovation, and climate change has spurred an unprecedented rate of transformation—both inside and outside our school districts (Friedman 2016). This accelerated pace of change is contributing to a growing sense of uncertainty and overwhelming pressure, especially for our district leaders.

The year 2007 introduced some of the greatest technological innovations in our history—innovations that have accelerated the pace of technological change. From the introduction of the iPhone, to the emergence of social media networks, 2007 gave rise to many of the technologies we see in our districts today. Next-generation learning management systems (LMS), iPads, cheaper and faster classroom devices, and digital content are just a few of the many innovations emerging from this period. While these innovations have unlocked new opportunities for transforming K–12 education, they are changing at a scope and rate that surpass our ability to adapt. Now, for the first time in our history, our districts are struggling to produce graduates with the competencies to thrive in a globally competitive world.

The pace of change and the availability of technological solutions have caused K–12 education to turn to single-point solutions. Single-point solutions are short-sighted responses to the common problems our school districts face. Unlike long-term, systemic solutions, single-point solutions are relatively fast and easy to implement—and thus are attractive given our hectic responsibilities as superintendents and leaders, our laundry list of competing priorities, and the changes occurring around us. If our teachers don't know how to teach in a digital environment, the seemingly obvious solution is to purchase professional learning. Or, if the problem seems to be the lack of laptop computers to support students, the obvious answer is to procure more devices. If the problem is housing

3

digital content and tracking performance, the obvious move is to purchase a learning management system. Single-point solutions often attempt to solve complicated problems with simple solutions—solutions that overlook the root of the problem, which is often hidden and systemic rather than visible and isolated.

Single-point solutions are ineffective because they target some, but not all the components of the education system needed for successful technology integration. For instance, leadership, the most fundamental factor in successful integration, is often overlooked or underemphasized. Technology initiatives often lack the direction of leadership, the buy-in and engagement of stakeholders, and the shared vision for the modern, or personalized, learning environment. Another overlooked area is instructional models. As districts procure technology, they often fail to redesign instructional and assessment models that are designed for an analog environment. Thus, these districts digitize traditional instruction, which leads to poor student outcomes. In the same vein, districts often procure technology without considering the need to change and standardize curriculum for the digital environment. Additionally, as districts procure more digital resources year after year, they often lack the ability to track, integrate, support, and sustain digital tools and content—not to mention optimize their use. Given the steep learning curve of teaching and assessing in a digital environment, districts often develop inadequate professional learning, which instructs teachers on the features and functions of new technology but fails to cover how to use it within the context of twenty-first century teaching practices. This professional learning also fails to adequately prepare school-based leaders to manage change or effectively assess teachers in a digital environment.

This is not the fault of our school districts; rather, it underscores the complexity and difficulty of this work. What is needed is a proven method and approach for transitioning our districts to modern learning environments.

DIGITAL CONVERGENCE: THE SOLUTION

The answer to the problems facing K–12 education is Digital Convergence. Digital Convergence is the fundamental change needed at both national and district levels to successfully integrate technology into classrooms and use it to transform the student learning experience. At the national level, Digital Convergence is the intersection of people and ideas as they seek a unified approach to transform the existing education system through technology adoption. At the school district level, Digital Convergence is the successful combination of five major drivers through which technology adoption can effectively occur—leadership, instructional models, modern curriculum, digital ecosystems, and professional learning—to redesign existing infrastructure and resources to support personalized learning. Only by engaging in the work of Digital Convergence can our industry capitalize on the potential of technology present in other sectors. As this book explores, Digital Convergence is technically simple, yet socially complex.

Digital Convergence Framework

The Digital Convergence Framework serves as a practical tool for your district to engage in the work of transitioning from the traditional classroom model to the modern learning environment. The framework encompasses seven stages across the five drivers of Digital Convergence and enables you to track your progress and see the interrelated work needed across many components of the education system. Each stage and driver contains success indicators, or action items, that demonstrate advancement toward Convergence. This book explores the first three stages of Digital Convergence and illustrates the early progress of districts beginning this important work.

I invite you to embark with me on the journey toward Digital Convergence.

PART I:

WHEN FAST GETS FASTER

In 2016, I traveled to over half the states in the US and spent time with thousands of superintendents, cabinet members, school-based leaders, and teachers to understand why the country's education system is struggling to replace the traditional classroom model. Consistently, I interacted with superintendents and educational leaders who felt overwhelmed. It didn't matter if they lived in Alaska or Texas; they expressed disbelief at the drastic changes occurring inside and outside their districts. Many longed for the past when life seemed less complex and tumultuous.

I grew up in the Midwest "Rust Belt," where my father worked for the same manufacturing company for 42 years before he retired and where his father worked before him. Today, all that remains of the factory is a rusted foundation where it once stood. I use this anecdote when I work with teachers, educational leaders, and community members from districts throughout the country. I ask participants to examine

> "...they expressed disbelief at the drastic changes occurring inside and outside their districts. Many longed for the past when life seemed less complex and tumultuous."

their past in an activity called "Through the Decades." It's meant to underscore the evolution of our communities and school districts over the years, as well as our ability to adapt to these changes.

I divide the participants into groups based on the decade in which they began serving in their school district or living in their community. Each group draws a T-Chart on a piece of paper. The left side of the chart pertains to the district's curriculum at the time, while the right side focuses on the community. I then ask them to reflect on that decade. Where did students go after graduation? What jobs were available? What companies formed the backbone of their communities? Inevitably the stories from the past begin to emerge and they realize with astonishment how the twentieth century's Industrial Revolution gave rise to the Information Age. They see how the curriculum matched the times and how public schools have answered the call to produce graduates with skills to compete in each respective era.

This exercise underscores our education system's historical ability to adapt to changes. Going from horsepower to steam power gave rise to the Industrial Revolution, just as the early years of the internet led to the Information Age and the dissemination of knowledge across the globe, consequently connecting geographically dispersed people and cultures. Human beings had 50 years to adapt to the Industrial Revolution. The move from the Industrial Revolution to the Information Age—the early internet—still gave human beings ample time to adapt to changes in technology.

In *Thank You For Being Late*, Thomas Friedman explores the major changes causing many to feel overwhelmed in

"Globalization, technology, and climate change are intersecting as major forces to accelerate the pace of change, preventing us from developing the appropriate systems to accommodate it."

today's world (Friedman 2016). Globalization, technology, and climate change are intersecting as major forces to accelerate the pace of change, preventing us from developing the appropriate systems to accommodate it. From a technological standpoint, Friedman points to a critical inflection point in 2007 that gave rise to a new breed of innovations. The iPhone was released, which caused Facebook, Twitter, and LinkedIn to reimagine their platforms. Followed by the rise of big data and analytics. The year 2007 created an acceleration of technological innovation that is consistent with futurist Ray Kurzweil's "Law of Accelerating Returns," which states "the rate of change in a wide variety of evolutionary systems (including but not limited to the growth of technologies) tends to increase exponentially" (Kurzweil 2000). Eight years later we see evidence with the rise of artificial intelligence (AI), human genome sequencing, and self-driving cars. On the horizon is a trip to Mars and beyond.

Consider a few of the many changes that have occurred in the K–12 education over this period. Next generation learning management systems (LMS) emerged, iPads proliferated, cheaper and faster classroom devices became the norm, and educational content turned digital. Today, as Kurzweil's

Law keeps pace—increasing exponentially—fast is getting really, really fast. As superintendents and educational leaders, it's why we feel like we are caught in this storm, overwhelmed and perplexed. It's not surprising many of us want to bury our heads in the

> **"Yet holding firm to the status quo will only accelerate our sense of being disoriented, frustrated, and powerless."**

sand and wait it out. As one superintendent told me, "I'm just trying to swim towards the eye of the storm." Yet holding firm to the status quo will only accelerate our sense of being disoriented, frustrated, and powerless. As we'll see, the only solution is to engage in thoughtful action.

11

The pressures we face as leaders are complex and numerous. Our school systems are overwhelmed by the sheer number of technology solutions available—solutions that target various components of our districts but fail to address other, equally important and interdependent areas. Our educators and stakeholders grow frustrated as our districts engage in an ever-repeating cycle of acquiring and then abandoning solutions after they fail to adequately meet the system's needs or bring about any meaningful or positive transformation. Our parents and students are increasingly questioning the paradigm of our traditional school systems, as technology continues to redefine their expectations and experiences in other segments of their lives. And across the country, our school districts are continually grappling with the clash between technology and the traditional processes, policies, and mental models of K–12 education. As K–12 education faces unprecedented uncertainty, the need for a more thoughtful and systematic approach to technology integration has never been more essential.

> "As K–12 education faces unprecedented uncertainty, the need for a more thoughtful and systematic approach to technology integration has never been more essential."

The conditions of our industry also complicate these pressures. State law requires students to attend K–12 schools for a specific age range, which ultimately guarantees a consistent demand for our school districts, minimizing the urgency to make immediate changes. Additionally, our industry operates with significant geographical constraints on access, as zoning laws determine the school students must attend if enrolling in a public institution. Our sector is also unionized in some parts of the country, presenting challenges for changing current policies, procedures, and components of the system. On top of that, governance structures at the federal, state, and local levels often compete. National foundations flex their points of view with grant monies, the publishing industry often dictates curriculum with their products, and higher education produces our nation's teaching force. Taken together these factors have reduced competition, created conflict of interests across various stakeholder groups, and increased adherence to the status quo, which for K–12 education means adhering to the traditional, teacher-centric classroom model—a model that prevents our districts from integrating technology meaningfully, effectively, or organically to transform teaching and learning for the modern age.

Considering the current state of K–12 education, and the opportunity afforded by technology, two fundamental questions arise: Why is K–12 education the last frontier in technology adoption? And more importantly, How can our school districts successfully transition from the traditional K–12 classroom model to modern, or personalized, learning environments? This book sets out to answer these and other questions by giving you a framework to help your school district navigate the disruption of technology integration occurring in K–12 education today.

The answer to the tentative state of K–12 education is Digital Convergence. Digital Convergence is the fundamental change needed at the national and school-district levels to successfully integrate

"Digital Convergence is the fundamental change needed at the national and school-district levels to successfully integrate technology into classrooms and use it to transform the student learning experience."

technology into classrooms and use it to transform the student learning experience. At the national level, Digital Convergence is the intersection of people and ideas as they seek a unified approach to transform the existing education system through technology adoption. At the school-district level, Digital Convergence is the successful combination of five major drivers of work through which technology adoption can effectively occur—leadership, instructional models, modern curriculum, digital ecosystems, and professional learning—to redesign existing infrastructure and resources to support modern learning. Only by engaging in the work of Digital Convergence can our industry capitalize on the potential of technology present in other sectors. As we'll see, Digital Convergence is technically simple, yet socially complex.

This book does not detail technological solutions or explore the in-depth changes occurring today in K–12 education. Instead, it serves as a practical guide for K–12 superintendents and leaders who, in accepting the need to transform their school districts through technology, find themselves overwhelmed by the number of solutions in the industry today, all of which promise to heal systemic problems with

"This book is for the leaders who are seeking a framework to approach technology integration more thoughtfully, systematically, and fundamentally."

single-point, near-sighted solutions—solutions that ignore the underlying causes of the problem and offer only temporary relief of symptoms. This book is for the leaders who are seeking a framework to approach technology integration more thoughtfully, systematically, and fundamentally. It's also for leaders seeking to understand systems and change management.

This book is for the leaders who feel like they're leading their districts and communities from inside a turbulent, unpredictable storm.

SINGLE-POINT SOLUTIONS: THE BARRIER TO MODERN LEARNING ENVIRONMENTS

The barriers to Digital Convergence—the process of transitioning your school district to modern learning environments—are *single-point solutions*. Single-point solutions come in many forms, the greatest of which is our natural inclination to think linearly and episodically. In many ways, our habits and even our language influence our direct approach to

> "The barriers to Digital Convergence—the process of transitioning your school district to modern learning environments—are *single-point solutions*."

addressing a problem, though oftentimes the root of the problem is rarely apparent and is based on multiple, interrelated factors—factors that are systemic and underlying rather than ancillary and easily identifiable. Given the rate of change in school districts and the sense of being overwhelmed, it's easy to see why single-point solutions are the pervasive choice in K–12. While these 1:1 solutions provide relief, any respite remains temporary, giving way to other, often greater problems and unforeseen consequences.

At their core, single-point solutions are short-sighted responses to the common challenges that our school districts face. If our teachers don't know how to teach in a digital environment, the seemingly obvious solution is to purchase professional learning. Or if the problem seems to be the lack of laptop computers to support students, the obvious answer is to procure more devices. If the problem is housing digital content and tracking performance, the obvious move is to purchase a learning management system.

But after making the purchase, what if the professional learning doesn't adequately reflect your district's unique pedagogical practices, curriculum, or technology environment, leaving teachers just as unprepared, and even more confused and frustrated?

Or what if the laptops are rarely used—or used ineffectively—because classrooms rely primarily on direct instruction, lesson plans and units of instruction don't support their use, teachers don't understand how to incorporate them into teaching and learning activities, or they remain unsupported from an IT perspective?

Or what if the learning management system can't support your existing digital resources, doesn't reflect your curriculum, is too complex for your teachers, or doesn't integrate with your pedagogical practices and assessment methods?

> "...the problems our school districts encounter are complex and dependent on multiple, interrelated factors that single-point solutions can't adequately address."

As these questions illustrate, the problems our school districts encounter are complex and dependent on multiple, interrelated factors that single-point solutions can't adequately address. Purchasing only one solution, or purchasing multiple and leaving them to vendors to manage separately, results in significant barriers to Digital Convergence. As previously illustrated, these single-point solutions often target some but not all the drivers needed for Digital Convergence, fail to address the drivers adequately, or disrupt the entire process of Digital Convergence.

As leaders implementing technology, it's often challenging to establish a shared vision when we face constant resistance from community members, teachers, and students. Additionally, other challenges include redesigning instructional models and curriculum to replace traditional practices. Adherence to traditional teaching methods prevents teachers and students from leveraging the full capability of technology, such as the ability to personalize and individualize learning, which would allow students to learn at their own pace, in their preferred style, according to their unique needs. Another problem is that devices are implemented without considering interoperability, thereby frustrating and fragmenting the teaching and learning experience. Another challenge is providing professional learning that effectively prepares teachers to perform in a modern environment and keep pace with technology, especially as roles, strategies, and pedagogies evolve.

Single-point solutions are ultimately a result of the lack of coordinated foresight, participation, and resources among all stakeholders affected by technology integration. Nowhere is this more apparent than between our school districts and schools. As school districts continue to struggle with managing budgets, many schools must make their own purchasing decisions as they convert from analog to digital. These schools often purchase solutions that address school-specific needs but are not supported at the district level, ultimately

> **"The only answer to single-point solutions is a unified approach to the selection, implementation, and integration of modern learning solutions."**

resulting in a fragmented learning network. This issue is further enhanced by the invention of new and innovative education technology, which has increased the need for informed choices when purchasing digital resources. The only answer to single-point solutions is a unified approach to the selection, implementation, and integration of modern learning solutions.

THE CASE OF THE SINGLE-POINT SOLUTION

Consider an example. Your district is in dire need for new devices, as the ratio of students to computers is currently 20:1. Recognizing this problem, your district makes a significant investment in 1:1 computing. The move promises to eliminate barriers to access and facilitate more personalized learning, giving teachers and students 24-7 access to instructional content anywhere there is an internet connection.

A week after deploying the devices, you hear minimal feedback, most of which is positive.

Another week passes. Still only minor feedback.

Another week passes. Now you discover a problem.

The bandwidth in some of your schools is not enough to support the increasing demand of using the devices. Teachers and students struggle to access the internet, causing frustration and disruptions throughout the course of the day.

And then you discover another problem.

In some classrooms, the devices are not being used at all. They sit on shelves collecting dust, as teachers return to more conventional forms of lecturing, practice, and review. After inquiring about why the devices are not being used, you learn about the inadequate training teachers are receiving. Focused solely on the features and functions of the technology, the training leaves teachers with no understanding of how to use the devices in the context of instruction. Many are frustrated and see the devices as a distraction, not a tool for effective teaching and learning.

And then another problem.

Student outcomes are growing worse in classrooms that are actively using the devices. You observe a lecture in one of the classrooms, where you quickly see the problem. The teacher stands at the helm of the classroom lecturing his students through a 50-slide PowerPoint deck, as students are following along on their tablets. Heads bobbing, eyes drowsy, attention shifting—you discover another issue: some teachers are merely digitizing the traditional classroom model.

And then more problems.

Other classes are using the devices during certain times of the day, typically after teachers have completed most of their lessons. You realize that teachers are struggling to create lesson plans that build rigor and higher-level thinking into a digital environment.

And more.

Frustration continues to rise among stakeholders. Students are frustrated. Parents are frustrated. Teachers are frustrated. Most see the investment as a poor decision, and many feel the district leadership should've consulted with the people who would be most

> **"Considering the number of solutions implemented in a given year, it's easy to gauge the financial, intellectual, psychological, and societal impact single-point solutions can have for a district."**

affected by the change before moving forward. Speaking with staff and teachers, it becomes apparent that many see the change as a threat to the status quo, while conversations with students and parents highlight their disappointment that the district doesn't provide a better learning experience through technology.

And so on.

This example illustrates the common consequences caused by single-point solutions, which in this case created several unforeseen problems. Considering the number of solutions implemented in a given year, it's easy to gauge the financial, intellectual, psychological, and societal impact single-point solutions can have for a district.

21

LEADERSHIP CHALLENGES

You face enormous challenges by nature of your position.

As a leader looking to transition your district to the modern learning environment, you face a status quo over a century in the making.

You face mental models and modes of thinking deeply-engrained and reinforced over multiple generations.

You face well-defined structures, systems, policies, and procedures that are difficult to change.

You face human emotions and self-perceptions defined by existing roles and responsibilities.

You face fear of the unknown and stakeholders who are by nature risk-averse.

You face other impediments to your vision, including those imposed by local, state, and federal government and other third parties.

> **"As a leader looking to transition your district to the modern learning environment, you face a status quo over a century in the making."**

The challenges specific to leadership are complex, but they are the most funda-mental in the transi-tion to modern learn-ing environments. No other area of work in K–12 education is more significant and important to ensuring districts can successfully navigate Digital Convergence to transform teaching and learning for the modern age.

Resistance to change is one of the greatest barriers you face to modern learning environments. Teachers, staff, parents, and other stakeholders often resist the transition to modern learning environments, and this resistance is amplified by their inability to understand, comprehend, and envision what the transition entails. Creating awareness around the initiative and providing routine communication are necessities for you and your district; however, they are often inhibited by the silos that naturally exist in school systems and the lack of a shared vocabulary for the changes that are occurring. Other factors that fuel uncertainty and skepticism include media coverage of inadequate teacher training and over-attention on technology as districts seek to modernize, as well as the track record of previous technology-integration initiatives, which were quickly abandoned after failing to meet the district's needs. Resistance is also driven by competing interests and general frustration over the number of local, state, and federal initiatives in which teachers and stakeholders must comply and participate.

Leadership challenges do not rest solely with you. School leaders often lack the knowledge of how to effectively manage the transition to modern learning environments, especially given the strength of the status quo and resistance

23

to change. These leaders require effective change management training to successfully engage with stakeholders and facilitate acceptance and ownership of the initiative.

Instructional Model Challenges

In addition to traditional leadership strategies, another barrier to modern learning environments is the methods by which we teach and assess our students.

Direct face-to-face instruction is, for the most part, the predominant pedagogy of our traditional classrooms. Throw in digital technology and the dynamic becomes inconsistent rather than aligned.

24

Consider the previous example of delivering a PowerPoint lecture via digital devices. The pedagogy remains the same (i.e., analog lecture) only now it is delivered through both analog and digital means. Research shows that simply digitizing traditional instruction invariably leads to lower levels of cognitive rigor.

Another barrier is the absence of model blended units of instruction that optimize instruction in a modern learning environment across the system. Some teachers may develop lesson plans that are effective in a digital learning space, but they remain only a small subset of the overall district curriculum. To support the clear majority of teachers in developing exemplars, what's needed is an industry standard by which we can measure the effectiveness of instructional design.

CURRICULUM CHALLENGES

Another challenge is curriculum. Traditional curriculum treats students the same in each grade level. A factory model of K–12 education, traditional curriculum shuttles students through a uniform process that determines what they learn, how they learn, and when they learn.

In this way, traditional curriculum follows a one-size-fits-all approach. Except for date of birth, traditional curriculum ignores the individual character-istics of the student, which include preferred learning style, strengths and weaknesses, and learning habits—all characteristics of a student's learning profile. A kinesthetic learner, for instance, is treated the same as students whose

> "A factory model of K–12 education, traditional curriculum shuttles students through a uniform process that determines what they learn, how they learn, and when they learn."

preferred method of learning is visual or verbal. In terms of strengths and weaknesses and academic readiness factors, a fourth-grade student who performs mathematics at a sixth-grade level and English at a second-grade level is required to learn at the same level as his or her peers. Additionally, a student who needs more time to learn and master concepts must follow the same pace as a fast-learning student—a pace that may be ineffective for both. Like pedagogy, traditional curriculum is designed for analog representation. What's needed is a shift toward a more modern curriculum.

In addition to the characteristics of learners, traditional curriculum largely ignores the outcomes of learning. Students demonstrate their learning through one means of representation, which may or may not reflect their preferred learning style and certainly doesn't reflect whether they've mastered their learning. Instead, students are assigned a grade, and like factory-produced commodities, shipped to the next phase on the continuum.

DIGITAL RESOURCE CHALLENGES

Other barriers to Digital Convergence reside in the digital resources themselves. Mainly, these problems come from a lack of integration

Imagine a storage room filled with unopened boxes containing new tablets, laptops, and gadgets. Despite a relatively recent date of purchase, you're surprised to discover that a coat of dust rests on top of each box, evidence suggesting the degree of neglect.

> **"The lack of integration ultimately creates a fragmented teaching and learning experience, requiring users to access digital resources via multiple points, necessitating duplicative tasks, and/or preventing the use of one or more digital resources."**

How about a complicated collection of digital content and resources with no clear path to identifying, inventorying, tracking, and supporting them?

How about notebooks filled with multiple user credentials and URLs that teachers and students regularly consult to access and interact with digital resources?

These symptoms naturally arise from the challenges districts encounter when procuring resources. Consider the case of purchasing from multiple vendors, who often provide disparate, standalone solutions. The lack of integration ultimately creates a fragmented teaching and learning experience, requiring users to access digital resources via multiple points, necessitating duplicative tasks, and/or preventing the use of one or more digital resources. These challenges are further complicated when digital resources behave differently than what was promised or demonstrated by vendors.

Another barrier is the use of all-in-one solutions, such as learning management systems. Despite their billing, these single-point solutions fail to meet the complete needs of teachers, students, and stakeholders. Oftentimes, the district's instructional model will require advanced features of a learning management system, such as requiring students to demonstrate mastery that might not exist yet in the product.

Given the amount of digital resources a district may procure, another barrier is ensuring resources provide the same look and feel to users. Resources tend to vary across grade level and even content areas, which further fragments the learning experience.

Depending on the size of the school district and its budget, the availability of digital resources may be disproportionate within the system. For instance, larger school districts often struggle to provide equitable access to digital resources across their schools. Some schools may enjoy 1:1 computing, whereas others may be less fortunate.

While digital resources and learning management systems comprise some of the digital challenges, other digital tools further complicate the digital dilemma. This becomes apparent when considering the various other tools and applications that interact with digital learning resources, such as Google Apps or a digital graphing calculator for an advanced calculus class. Seem all too familiar? Districts around the country are wrestling with creating a solution that looks, feels, and acts like it was designed as a standalone resource.

PROFESSIONAL LEARNING CHALLENGES

Assume that you have effectively raised awareness, fostered engagement, and garnered participation in the movement toward modern learning environments. You've also initiated the effort to transform pedagogy and build exemplar lesson plans and units of instruction. You're tackling the problem of traditional curriculum by empowering the right stakeholders to redesign curriculum through a modern lens. And by delegating to another group of stakeholders, you're beginning to reevaluate and redesign how digital resources, digital tools, and learning management systems are procured, integrated, supported, and sustained.

Yet what is the value of these efforts if there is no consistent, reliable, and scalable means to help teachers instruct within the context of the new curriculum, digital resources and tools, and pedagogical practices? Or a thoughtful and meaningful way to inform principals on the factors that distinguish effective from ineffective teaching in these modern learning environments? Or if there is no means to educate staff on the nuances of the modern learning environment so they may intelligibly and effectively interact with parents and community members?

Professional learning, despite its importance, remains a pain point for many districts. Teachers rarely receive education beyond the features and functions of new technology. Driven oftentimes from vendor-supported training, this instruction lacks deep inquiry from participants; creates an isolated and disconnected experience; and lacks any meaningful application, practice, and feedback from participants themselves.

> "Professional learning, despite its importance, remains a pain point for many districts."

One cause of such ineffective training is the traditional paradigm of professional learning. Like students, teachers and other stakeholders are often confined to one mode of learning, which fails to accommodate diverse learning styles and preferences. Rather than self-paced learning, professional education is often front- and back-loaded during the school year, which in turn reduces teachers' retention and engagement. It's difficult not to feel mentally exhausted by the end of the school year, a time when many districts require teachers to attend mandatory professional learning days that cover content many will forget over summer break. While engagement will likely improve when professional learning is delivered at the

30

start of the school year, many teachers will still struggle to retain their learning.

Professional learning in districts also pose challenges to delivering instruction in an accessible, repeatable, and consistent manner. Often delivered in a face-to-face setting, the quality and consistency of learning varies by instructor, cannot be consistently reproduced, and is difficult to make up if missed. Professional learning for new hires suffers from these same limitations. Ultimately, onboarding programs fail to provide new teachers and staff with timely, accessible, repeatable, consistent, and effective role-specific education.

Notably, the traditional paradigm of professional learning reinforces the model imposed on students. To effectively make the transition to modern learning environments, teachers, staff, and other stakeholders need education designed for the twenty-first century.

> "Rather than self-paced learning, professional education is often front- and back-loaded during the school year, which in turn reduces teachers' retention and engagement."

31

32

PART II:

DIGITAL CONVERGENCE

THE DIGITAL CONVERGENCE REVOLUTION
(HOW IT ALL STARTED)

To understand Digital Convergence and the journey ahead, we must reflect on our progress to date.

At the turn of the century, technology served an auxiliary purpose in K–12 education. Computers and other devices were largely relegated to activities outside of daily instruction. In these early years, the most fundamental barrier to technology integration was access, as most classrooms lacked enough computers to support student learning. In 2000, for instance, the ratio of students to instructional computers was 6.6:1 (National Center for Education Statistics 2010), and only 77 percent of school districts reported having access to the internet (Wells and Lewis 2006, 4). Another limitation was the functionality of the internet, which offered few advantages over the predominant traditional classroom resources such as textbooks (Greenhow, Robelia, and Hughes 2016, 246-259). Termed "Web 1.0," this early version of the internet allowed users to consume knowledge offered

> **"Yet within a few years, as the pace of technological innovation accelerated, K–12 leaders, educators, and innovators began to glimpse the possibilities of the modern learning environment."**

34

by a few content providers but made creating and sharing information difficult.

Yet within a few years, as the pace of technological innovation accelerated, K–12 leaders, educators, and innovators began to glimpse the possibilities of the modern learning environment (Greenhow, Robelia, and Hughes 2016, 246-259). In 2004, the introduction of Web 2.0 gave way to a new paradigm where users could create and share content, as well as collaborate with other users, just as easily as they could consume information. The internet soon flooded with content in various forms, such as blogs, podcasts, and videos; social networking sites that enabled users to connect and engage; and collaborative content creation sites like wikis that enabled users to post and share knowledge in their area of expertise. Soon, the potential of Web 2.0 to transform the traditional model of education was apparent, and our industry began to take notice.

At this point, the rate of technological change was still manageable. School districts around the country began investing millions of dollars in one of the first technologies that promised to transform teaching and learning for the

> **"School districts around the country began investing millions of dollars in one of the first technologies that promised to transform teaching and learning for the twenty-first century."**

twenty-first century. Smart boards, or interactive white boards (IWBs), offered to substitute direct, face-to-face instruction with a more interactive and engaging method of teaching—a method that would accommodate various learning styles and replace the factory model of traditional K–12 education (Higgins, Beauchamp, Miller 2007, 213-225). While expensive, IWBs would allow teachers to access a range of multimedia—such as videos, internet resources, and pictures—and enrich the learning experience for students. They would also encourage student participation and engagement by enabling students to interact with the IWBs and their various content. Furthermore, IWBs would make it easy to save and revisit past lessons, enabling teachers to solidify concepts and provide a more seamless learning experience. IWBs would also enable teachers to collaborate and share lesson plans outside of classroom hours—and therefore increase the efficiency, productivity, and quality of instruction.

For the first time, IWBs would provide a glimpse into the true barriers to effective technology integration and the impediments of the modern learning environment. Teachers received inadequate professional learning, which became evident as they struggled to incorporate IWBs into their daily instruction and use the technology interactively. Teachers who used the technology did so through a teacher-centric model of instruction, which often confused students with the presentation of information. The IWBs also posed ergonomic problems as the technology could not accommodate the different heights of teachers and students. Other problems included difficulty maintaining the equipment and setting it up for classroom use. In many ways, these early challenges foreshadowed some of today's challenges that prevent districts from transitioning to modern learning environments.

Despite the failure of these early technology investments, our industry continued to make significant investments in technology and infrastructure. By 2005, nearly 100 percent of school districts had access to the internet, a 23 percent increase from only five years before (Wells and Lewis 2006, 4). Of those school districts, 97 percent offered broadband. The ratio of students to instructional computers also continued to decline to 3.8:1 by 2005. Handheld devices also began proliferating, with 19 percent of school districts offering them to students—a 10 percent increase from two years before. Districts also started programs to lend laptop computers to students. Additionally, to accommodate the influx of new technology, districts began offering

"Then came 2007 and a new age of innovation."

more professional learning in-person and online. By 2005, 83 percent of school districts offered professional learning programs on new technology.

Then came 2007 and a new age of innovation. As Friedman argues, this year led to generations of technology that would make it increasingly easier for consumers to "connect, collaborate, and create throughout every aspect of life" (Friedman 2016). It would also make it possible to digitize a broader set of elements and processes—whether educational content or the model of the traditional classroom. After 2007, we would see the emergence of the next generation of learning management systems (LMS), the proliferation of iPads and classroom devices that were cheaper and faster to use, the influx of digital content and resources, and more.

In 2009, the ratio of students to computers would continue to fall (Gray, Thomas, Lewis 2010). The BYOD ("bring your own device") movement would decrease the ratio of students to computers to 1.7:1. The uses of technology would also dramatically expand from just nine short years before. School districts began using technology to enable students to collaborate in school, contribute to blogs and wikis, use social networking sites, and more. With the

> **"...we would see the emergence of the next generation of learning management systems (LMS), the proliferation of iPads and classroom devices that were cheaper and faster to use, the influx of digital content and resources, and more."**

adoption of technology in other areas outside the school system, most districts also recognized the importance of technology in schools, with 88 percent identifying it as a key priority. With significant investments made in technology, 78 percent of districts reported having the adequate infrastructure to support its use. Additionally, 83 percent reported that teachers wanted to use technology in the classroom. These data represent a dramatic evolution in how K–12 leaders, educators, and students perceived technology and its role in the classroom—an evolution driven by technology's growing role in every aspect of daily life. Despite this acceptance of technology and urgency around its integration, significant barriers remained. For instance, only 58 percent of districts reported that teachers were adequately trained to integrate technology effectively in their instruction.

In 2010, K–12 education would face stringent budget cuts as the US still struggled in the wake of the Great Recession (Hull 2010). While the Great Recession took place in 2008 and 2009, most school districts overcame its effects by cutting nonessential expenditures like travel and energy costs. By 2010, however, districts would need to make more significant cuts by laying off teachers, reducing professional learning, and eliminating other programs. The Great Recession would further delay our progress toward the modern learning environment.

Today, our industry stands ready and capable of

adapting to our turbulent environment to transform teaching and learning for the modern age. As K–12 education technology has grown to a multi-billion-dollar industry, and innovation continues its dizzying pace, some school districts are demonstrating significant progress

> "Today, our industry stands ready and capable of adapting to our turbulent environment to transform teaching and learning for the modern age."

in overcoming the turbulence. These districts are making strides toward establishing the modern learning environment—proof that other districts can and should engage in this vital work. Our hearts and minds are in the right place, and we've universally bought in to technology's importance in the K–12 classroom. Yet for our industry to collectively take a step forward—to begin the journey toward Digital Convergence— we must approach this effort courageously, systematically, thoughtfully, and collaboratively.

I invite you to embark with me on the journey to Digital Convergence.

40

DIGITAL CONVERGENCE DEFINED

Digital Convergence is the fundamental movement needed to transform our traditional classrooms into modern learning environments. This
change exists on two
fronts. Nationally, Digi-
tal Convergence repre-
sents the unification of
the ideas and efforts of
K–12 leaders, innova-

> **"Digital Convergence is the fundamental movement needed to transform our traditional classrooms into modern learning environments."**

tors, and educators as they collectively seek to overcome the
barriers to technology adoption and advance the progress of
our industry. For your school district, Digital Convergence
represents systematic work across five key components of the
education system needed to successfully implement, support,
and sustain the modern learning environment. These components, or drivers of Digital Convergence, include leadership,
instructional models, modern curriculum, digital ecosystems,
and professional learning. Through systematic and ongoing
work in these areas, your district can overcome the barriers
that prevented you from integrating technology previously.

As discussed in Part I, the barriers to the modern learning environment exist in the form of single-point solutions,
which target some but not all the components of the education system needed for effective technology integration. IWBs,

41

for instance, became single-point solutions because of how districts approached their implementation. Districts lacked unified direction, engagement, participation, and governance to promote, structure, support, and oversee IWB use. Pedagogy and assessment models remained designed for the traditional classroom, which conflicted with the technology and led to poor student outcomes. Curriculum was also designed for traditional instruction and thus led to inconsistent and ineffective uses of the technology. IWBs and other resources remained disparate and lacked the infrastructure and support to provide easy access and a seamless user experience. Furthermore, teachers lacked the professional training to effectively incorporate the technology in their instruction. Districts approached IWBs linearly as a plug-and-play solution despite their effects across the major components of the education system.

Digital Convergence follows a dynamic and iterative journey, unlike the linear path of a single-point solution. As work in one area of Digital Convergence advances, your district must simultaneously address the other components of the education system to sustain and support technology integration.

"As work in one area of Digital Convergence advances, your district must simultaneously address the other components of the education system to sustain and support technology integration."

The interrelation among the components of the education system is best described by Jay Forrester and Peter Senge, who developed a language in the form of archetypes to describe how systems interact as solutions are applied to them (Braun 2002). Forrester and Senge's findings illustrate the need for a solution that solves fundamental problems and provides foresight to the people implementing them. Because a complex system contains a myriad of interrelations among system components, the input on the system is dependent on numerous conditions. Comprehensive solutions that facilitate Digital Convergence allow coordination among components and address all conditions required to make the solution successful. These dynamic solutions encourage stakeholders to view their effect on the entire system, rather than viewing their effect on an isolated part of the system.

43

Additionally, Digital Convergence ensures that digital assets provide sustainable value over time by making sure that the solution continues to adequately meet the needs of each part of the system. This prevents the solution from becoming obsolete

> **"Digital Convergence is not a destination, but a state that is continuously changing amid changes in technology and each of the five drivers of the education system."**

for failing to integrate with one part of the education system.

Digital Convergence is not a destination, but a state that is continuously changing amid changes in technology and each of the five drivers of the education system. The highly dynamic nature of Digital Convergence necessitates that you establish an assessment process or framework to measure your district's progress. It also requires that you leverage technology to help track and anticipate barriers to Digital Convergence, such as using predictive analytics to understand trends and allocate resources to effectively integrate technology.

THE 5 DRIVERS OF DIGITAL CONVERGENCE

For Digital Convergence to successfully occur, the work of your districts must span these five components.

··· Leadership ···

As discussed in Part I, leadership serves as the most important and fundamental driver of twenty-first century teaching and learning. This vital area of work begins with you. To keep leadership engaged, it is important to set the direction for the overall movement, invite stakeholders to establish a shared vision, and facilitate stakeholder

> "...leadership serves as the most important and fundamental driver of twenty-first century teaching and learning."

44

involvement. Another important area of focus includes creating an effective governance structure, along with formal processes and an interdisciplinary team to manage, support, and oversee the work—ensuring it remains reflective of the values, preferences, and needs of stakeholders.

··· Instructional Models ···

The instructional model is the second important area of work for Digital Convergence. This work entails the translation of instructional pedagogy and assessments from the traditional space to the modern, digital learning environment. To ensure proper management, alignment, and support of the instructional model, this driver necessitates the creation and ongoing collaboration of a cross-functional team. It also requires a framework for assessing instructional rigor and twenty-first-century skills, the development of learning profiles, and more. The instructional model ensures that instruction provides blended, personalized learning that is rigorous, relevant, and relational to prepare students for the twenty-first century.

··· Modern Curriculum ···

Next is the modern curriculum. This serves as the sequence and scope of instructional content through which students develop twenty-first-century skills and competencies. Unlike traditional curriculum that offers a one-size-fits-all approach, modern curriculum facilitates highly personalized

45

and individualized learning—allowing students to choose when, where, and how they learn. Modern curriculum is a fundamental component of Digital Convergence that requires the development of a blended unit plan, the assessment of all digital content, opportunities for students to create content rather than passively consume it, and more.

··· Digital Ecosystem ···

With the influx of digital resources, another vital area of work pertains to developing, supporting, and sustaining the digital ecosystem. A digital ecosystem is the foundational infrastructure through which teachers and students access digital resources relevant to their roles and responsibilities. The digital ecosystem ensures all digital resources are integrated and supported, and users follow a seamless, tailored experience as they access and interact with its interwoven elements. The digital ecosystem is supported through a shared vision, governance structure, formal processes, and the work of interdisciplinary teams—all ensuring that the ecosystem incorporates the values, preferences, and needs of users over time.

> "With the influx of digital resources, another vital area of work pertains to developing, supporting, and sustaining the digital ecosystem."

··· Professional Learning ···

The final area of work is professional learning. This work ensures that teachers and other stakeholders develop the necessary skills, competencies, and pedagogy to transform teaching and learning for the twenty-first century. Effective professional learning guarantees that teachers can integrate technology into classroom instruction and effectively facilitate and assess personalized and competency-based learning. This driver represents a foundational element to Digital Convergence that requires a long-term strategic plan, the development and support of a cross-functional team, and systems to develop, deploy, and monitor professional learning for teachers and other stakeholders. Finally, it seeks to measure teacher proficiency with the new instructional model and technology integration, rather than just attendance at the training.

DIGITAL CONVERGENCE FRAMEWORK

The Digital Convergence Framework is a tool to help you and your district approach and engage in this work. The framework is designed to guide your district in its journey toward Digital Convergence, while supporting your leadership decisions, providing you with a strategic mindset, and identifying the critical questions you must consider. The framework identifies a series of important action items, called success indicators, across the five drivers of Digital Convergence at the district level. The framework is not intended to serve as a prescriptive formula. I've found that great leaders approach the framework systematically, question how each area of work interrelates, and develop interdisciplinary teams to oversee and execute the work of each driver.

> "The Digital Convergence Framework is a tool to help you and your district approach and engage in this work."

Digital Convergence, The Early Years: Stages 1-3

This book explores the first three stages of Digital Convergence across each driver, which illustrate the early and emerging progress of districts engaged in this work. For instance, you learn about the critical action items that occur in Stage 1, 2, and 3 of leadership. Part III of this book explores each stage in detail across the five areas of work and provides insight into the various success indicators that indicate advancement in a specific area. Success indicators encourage your district to approach Digital Convergence in a comprehensive, systematic manner, with each action item interdependent and requiring the collective participation

THE NEW AGENDA

and oversight of stakeholders in all areas of Digital Convergence. Because of the interrelation among the five areas of work and their respective success indicators, progress through the stages of Digital Convergence should remain relatively uniform, with your district demonstrating the most advancement in the category of leadership. That's because your work is fundamental to the modern learning environment and lays the foundation for the collective journey.

> "...progress through the stages of Digital Convergence should remain relatively uniform, with your district demonstrating the most advancement in the category of leadership."

49

50

PART III:

TRANSITIONING TO MODERN LEARNING ENVIRONMENTS

CONCEPTS OF DIGITAL CONVERGENCE

··· Tone from the Top ···

Over the last several years I have had the privilege to facilitate leadership forums on Digital Convergence with hundreds of educational leaders from across the country. Packed into a room for two and a half days, we embark on exciting and energetic discussions about the future of education, the role of technology, and the type of leadership needed for success. At some point, I change the conversation to ask an important question of my superintendent audience. In the context of Digital Convergence, I ask whether they believe they have the power and authority to transition traditional classrooms into modern learning environments. Surprisingly, most believe they don't.

In our research over the last few years, my colleagues and I have found this response as a significant differentiator between superintendents—not to mention their school districts. As we've studied leaders navigating the often murky waters of Digital Convergence, we've found that the success of the transition largely depends on the degree to which superintendents believe they have the power to

> **"...the success of the transition largely depends on the degree to which superintendents believe they have the power to influence it."**

influence it. Those who don't believe often point to the competing interests within their district and community. They point to complex governance structures coupled with teachers' unions and school boards. They point to state legislators and federal accountability laws that seem divorced from the everyday happenings of the classroom. They often cite local universities that lag behind cutting-edge teaching methods and a publishing industry dominated by profit margins. These conditions, they argue, make them nearly powerless to move their district forward.

Power exists in both the business and social sectors; the trick is knowing where to find it. Our research has shown that what differentiates some superintendents was where they found the power to move their districts forward. These visionaries were unwavering in their commitment to transform the educational environment in their districts. Yet the power didn't come from their own drive and determination. Instead, it came from the inclusion of stakeholders in constructing the path forward—in communication, shared interests, a common identity, and coalition building.

Making the transition from a traditional classroom model to a modern learning environment requires fundamental changes across the school system. Superintendents and principals must change the way they lead, curriculum writers how they design, teachers the way they teach, students the way they learn, and parents how they perceive and monitor

53

> **"The transition requires both a complete overhaul of how the traditional school system is designed and how staff are trained, but also how people fundamentally perceive the teaching and learning experience."**

their child's education. The transition requires both a complete overhaul of how the traditional school system is designed and how staff are trained, but also how people fundamentally perceive the teaching and learning experience. In the transition to modern learning environments, all stakeholders must embrace the new mental model and paradigm of twenty-first-century education.

This is no simple task for any leader. Change on a systemic scale naturally faces obstacles. Habits are entrenched and people are comfortable in the present way of doing things. Resources are scarce and the capital, time, or talent needed to make the transition requires disinvestment elsewhere. Personal feelings are attached to the people and processes that are likely to change—all impeding the transition toward Digital Convergence. Yet the superintendent must not be afraid to engage with those obstacles.

Given the challenges of Digital Convergence, the work toward building a modern learning environment naturally begins with the superintendent. The superintendent holds the position of highest authority and is perceived as the leader of the school system by internal and external stakeholders. He or she must lead the effort toward Digital Convergence by communicating the need for change, gaining the participation and buy-in of key stakeholders, and starting the development of a strategic plan to guide the overall journey.

> "...the work toward building a modern learning environment naturally begins with the superintendent."

Setting the direction for your district is not a team sport. The tone, message, and aspirational direction is set by you, the leader. This is clear when we recall the words of John F. Kennedy and his historical address to put a man on the moon by the end of the decade. Coming from the President of the United States, the direction was clear, and what remained was figuring out how to turn the vision into a reality. Kennedy needed the engagement from a myriad of stakeholders to see his plan come into fruition—stakeholders that included legislators, scientists, engineers, and philanthropists. While these later collaborative efforts were vital to the eventual moon landing in 1969, the mission's success began with the act of establishing the direction. The ability to transition to modern learning environments requires the same foundational starting point that Kennedy followed in 1961.

55

··· The Irony of Instruction (It's About the Learner) ···

For nearly a century, K–12 education has been designed to efficiently move students through the system on a massive scale. To achieve this, it has operated like a factory, treating students as identical in terms of learning styles, preferences, and readiness factors. To continue operating at an efficient pace, this model has evaluated students against one set of criteria and assigned grades that fail to accurately reflect students' mastery of their learning. In other words, traditional education has centered on what students are taught, not how students learn best.

> "...traditional education has centered on what students are taught, not how students learn best."

With the advent of technology, the boundaries that once prevented personalized and individualized learning on a massive scale are now surmountable. Technology has led to unprecedented access to information; content creation, sharing, and publication; and various means of consuming, creating, and representing knowledge. While the twentieth century focused predominately on what students were taught, the twenty-first century promises a new paradigm shift to focus on the learner, rather than the subject matter. Central to the creation of modern learning environments is the development and support of learner profiles, which detail the unique learn-

56

ing habits, preferences, and styles of students, including their strengths and weaknesses. This profile informs the teaching and learning experience. As neuroscience continues to identify the characteristics that most impact how we learn, several are shown to have a significant influence:

- Learning styles
- Intelligence preferences
- Academic readiness factors
- Gender
- Culture
- Language
- Emotion
- Personality

Consider the list above and what David Hood calls the paradigm of one: "one teacher, teaching one subject to one class of one age, using one curriculum at one pace, in one classroom, for one hour" (Hood 2015). This list alone would suggest that one student's unique learner profile has more than 40,000 neuropathways that affect how he or she learns at any moment. Multiply that by a class of 25 and it becomes clear why the conversation has focused on instruction – the *what*, not *who* of education – for the last 200 years.

Ultimately, technology has shifted the focal point from the teacher to the student. The teacher no longer serves as the sole source of instruction and knowledge. In the new modern learning environment, the student enjoys control over creating knowledge in the manner most effective for him or her to represent it, rather than passively consuming knowledge controlled by the teacher. In this new paradigm, the teacher shifts from the role of instructor to that of facilitator—guiding students along their individual learning paths to ensure optimal learning outcomes. Effective teachers relinquish the ownership of learning to their students and make teaching about the unique needs of each learner.

> **"Ultimately, technology has shifted the focal point from the teacher to the student."**

58

··· Crowd Source Content, Not Competencies ···

Technology and the internet have given way to information access, creation, and sharing at an unprecedented scale. Leaders, educators, and staff can now create and share lesson plans with colleagues and other pedagogues locally, regionally, and nationally. The removal of boundaries in time and space has created an opportunity to make curriculum development easier, faster, and more efficient for teachers and staff. It also promises to increase the quality of curriculum.

To optimize curriculum, however, your district must strive to develop the appropriate competencies that hold students accountable and ensure they have achieved the optimal knowledge, skills, and abilities at graduation. This requires your district to work internally and collaboratively to develop a knowledge map across the spectrum of K–12 learning that defines what every student should know and be able to do. Given the wealth of information at the disposal of teachers and staff, this knowledge

"...your district must strive to develop the appropriate competencies that hold students accountable and ensure they have achieved the optimal knowledge, skills, and abilities at graduation."

map optimizes the scope and consistency of learning and provides each individual learner with a dashboard showcasing progress against the competencies. Over time, it will also link crowd-sourced and district-created content to the map.

··· A Living, Breathing Habitat ···

A natural habitat offers the ideal conditions for organisms to thrive. Shelter from the elements, food, protection from predators, other symbiotic organisms—a habitat serves as a supportive network that meets the various needs of its diverse inhabitants. In many ways, K–12 education needs an analogous habitat to unify its digital resources and create the conditions to support and optimize the experiences of students, teachers, and other stakeholders.

Education technology is now a multi-billion-dollar industry that promises only to grow. As new technologies and vendors continue to emerge at an unprecedented rate, school districts are discovering great opportunity and headache given the sheer number of solutions available. On the one hand, the rise of innovation is leading to new possibilities for transforming teaching and learning for the modern age. On the other, the accelerated rate of technological change is creating significant challenges for districts as they struggle to integrate disparate assets. Thus, districts have turned to vendors selling all-in-one solutions that fail to adequately meet their needs, or have abandoned technologies in frustration as they acquire more resources year after year.

> "...districts have turned to vendors selling all-in-one solutions that fail to adequately meet their needs, or have abandoned technologies in frustration as they acquire more resources year after year."

Unfortunately, no single vendor or solution can provide districts with a fully-integrated, -supportive, and -functional ecosystem that meets the need of its inhabitants. Districts must work to build their own ecosystem organically and develop the internal processes, support systems, and infrastructure to sustain the ecosystem over time. This entails establishing a mission for the ecosystem; developing its own brand and communication outlet(s); creating a tiered and cross-functional team that includes executive sponsors and workgroups; establishing an implementation and ongoing maintenance plan; and creating protocols and workflows for vendor selection, technology integration, etc. In essence, districts must commit to developing a living, breathing ecosystem that facilitates interaction among a myriad of elements and reflects the needs of users now and in the future.

··· Inquiry, Then Proficiency, Not Attendance ···

Traditional professional learning programs focus on seat time. This system assumes that by attending a professional learning event, all teachers gain the same breadth and depth of new knowledge—knowledge that translates to their performance in the classroom. In this respect, traditional professional learning functions analogously to a factory; like products, teachers are treated universally the same without consideration of the unique learning styles, preferences, or abilities that determine learning outcomes. The design of the system evaluates teachers' proficiency based on seat time, rather than their ability to apply their learning proficiently in their role.

> "...teachers require more professional learning than ever to keep pace with changes created by an influx of new technology."

Today, teachers require more professional learning than

ever to keep pace with changes created by an influx of new technology. At the same time, teachers also need a new model for professional learning that makes learning more accessible, relevant, consistent, and accommodating. In this new model, teachers learn by creating an environment of peer collaboration and inquiry. The district needs to create the conditions for teachers to freely take risks, explore their intellectual curiosity about their practice with colleagues, and become reflective about their progression from a traditional classroom to a modern learning environment. As the culture of the district shifts towards teacher inquiry, specified and explicit outcomes of practice are defined, measured, and tracked for proficiency.

The modern learning environment calls for a new professional learning paradigm, one equally transformative and fundamental to the changes students are encountering. Because teachers facilitate the modern learning environment, it only makes sense that they experience it firsthand from a learner's perspective. This requires districts to provide teachers with the same personalized and individualized learning track afforded to students. Unlike the old completion requirement of seat time, the new paradigm provides teachers with inquiry-based learning and requires them to demonstrate proficiency. This increases the retention and practicality of professional learning, ensuring that teachers can operate effectively.

THE FRAMEWORK: STAGES I-III OF
DIGITAL CONVERGENCE

Digital Convergence follows a non-linear path. The interconnected nature of Digital Convergence often requires you to approach this work systematically and dynamically. While leadership efforts must begin and continue to lead the transition to modern learning environments, work in other areas may occur simultaneously and in no particular order. As mentioned before, it's important that you focus on the five drivers nonlinearly and seek to understand how each area of work interrelates. It's also important that you form interdisciplinary teams and ensure that stakeholders throughout the organization can speak to the vision and journey of Digital Convergence.

> "The interconnected nature of Digital Convergence often requires you to approach this work systematically and dynamically."

SUCCESS INDICATORS: THE BUILDING BLOCKS
OF CONVERGENCE

The Digital Convergence Framework includes success indicators, or action items, that indicate advancement in each driver and stage of Digital Convergence. The following section identifies the success indicators contained in Stages 1-3.

> "Success indicators encourage your district to approach Digital Convergence in a comprehensive, systematic manner."

Success indicators encourage your district to approach Digital Convergence in a comprehensive, systematic manner. Each success indicator is interdependent and therefore requires the collective participation and oversight of stakeholders in all five drivers of Digital Convergence.

64

THE JOURNEY BEGINS

Now that you are familiar with the concept of Digital Convergence, what's next? How do you engage this work? As the leader of your district, how do you move forward? Let's review each of the three stages of Digital Convergence across its five drivers.

STAGE 1

LEADERSHIP
STAGE 1

Over the years, I have helped hundreds of leaders, educators, and other stakeholders begin the journey toward Digital Convergence—experiences that have illustrated a common pattern for those approaching this work. Often, stakeholders inquire about the common characteristics of districts at this stage in the process. While they may be offering some degree of personalized learning, these districts lack the coordination to realize the full potential of the modern learning environment. Technology use is highly fragmented and inconsistent across the district, as individual teachers and administrators make decisions about digital tools and content. Moreover, the district lacks a unified instructional model that supports technology integration and pedagogical practices that are relevant in 2017. Teachers, staff, and stakeholders feel overwhelmed by the sheer number of digital resources and initiatives the district is implementing. Stakeholders find it difficult to understand how these changes impact their daily work, such as classroom practices. Ultimately, the district lacks a sense of

> "While they may be offering some degree of personalized learning, these districts lack the coordination to realize the full potential of the modern learning environment."

66

direction, cohesiveness, and coordination.

The journey toward Digital Convergence naturally begins with your leadership. At this stage in the process, your school district begins developing a *theory of action* for Digital Convergence. You also begin engaging stakeholders in the process—fostering conversations, awareness, and buy-in—as you seek to develop a plan for approaching this work. A fully developed, systemic plan occurs in the later stages of leadership; meanwhile, your teachers and administrators continue to make individual decisions about the use of technology tools, digital content, and instructional resources and models in their classrooms.

Success Indicator #1:

Set the Direction and Invite Stakeholders into the Process

Your district's journey toward modern learning environments begins when you set the direction to transform teaching and learning through technology. As the leader of your district, you must establish the need for change and create a sense of urgency to engage in this work. After setting the direction,

> **"Your district's journey toward modern learning environments begins when you set the direction to transform teaching and learning through technology."**

you must encourage others to participate in the formation of what the change will entail and invite stakeholders to co-construct the vision of the modern learning environment. Setting the direction individually eliminates competing interests and differing opinions. Inviting stakeholders into the process ensures that they are positioned to own, promote, and defend the movement rather than inhibit it.

After setting the direction, the next critical step is to invite stakeholders into the process. The need is apparent when one considers the sense of loss often associated with transitions. In *Managing Transitions: Making the Most of Change*, William Bridges discusses the three natural transitions people experience when responding to any change: "1. Letting go of the old ways and the old identity people had . . . 2. Going through an in-between time when the old is gone and the new isn't fully operational . . . 3. Coming out of the transition and making a new beginning" (Bridges 2009). According to Bridges, people moving through this transition period must gradually give up their previous identities—often a difficult, painful, and personal process. It's the role of the superintendent to empower principals to guide stakeholders through this transition period, keeping them informed, involved, and prepared.

Consider this question for a moment: "*Kids learn best when...?*" How would you answer that question? How would your leadership team answer it? How would your teachers, parents, and community answer it?

This shared vision is different from the overall district vision; it is a vision of the modern learning environment—including a mission and purpose for the work of Digital Convergence—that serves as a collective understanding and governs and informs all decisions going forward. This includes decisions made and work completed in each

> **"Important to the vision is a description of the district's desired future state of learning, as well as its core purpose."**

of the other areas of Digital Convergence—emphasizing the importance of leadership to drive the fundamental change.

Important to the vision is a description of the district's desired future state of learning, as well as its core purpose. The vision should set forth an agreed-upon destination that excites and motivates all stakeholders and ensures complete alignment.

··· Get everyone talking ···

To get everyone talking, start with *why*. Superintendents should begin by clearly defining the reasons for engaging in the work toward Digital Convergence. All stakeholders, internal and external to the school system, must understand the reasons behind the transition in order to fully embrace it. The reasons for the change should center on improving student learning and outcomes—ensuring students can develop twenty-first-century skills to contribute to a world that is both technologically and globally competitive.

Also important is addressing the negative connotations associated with the transition. Media coverage of districts may focus myopically on technology and neglect teacher training, causing educators and other stakeholders to potentially question or resist the transition. You should address these concerns directly by defining the transformation in terms of what it does and does not entail. You should highlight that the failures of past initiatives serve as lessons informing your district's efforts. Additionally, you should emphasize that the work of Digital Convergence is not about technology, but rather transforming teaching and learning for better outcomes, which involves all aspects of the school system working in unison. Simon Sinek, author of *Start with Why*, discusses the power of explaining the reason behind actions. According to Sinek, communicating the *why* over the *what* or *how* facilitates sustainable engagement and inspiration (Sinek 2009). Unlike superficial messaging, or messaging based on manipulation, clearly articulating the reasons for a change promotes feelings of loyalty, encouraging listeners to accept, embrace, and promote the change. William Bridges

> **"...superintendents must clearly outline why the movement to Digital Convergence is both necessary and vital."**

affirms this thesis when he writes, "You need to explain the purpose behind the new beginning clearly. . . you need to 'sell the problems' before you try to sell a solution to those problems" (Bridges 2009). Thus, superintendents must clearly outline why the movement to Digital Convergence is both necessary and vital.

> "Superintendents, before giving the why talk, must make a list of key internal and external stakeholders to include in the dialogue."

••• Know your stakeholders •••

Communicating the *why* is only one part of the equation. Who's involved in the conversation is another, equally important consideration. Superintendents, before giving the *why* talk, must make a list of key internal and external stakeholders to include in the dialogue. Though not comprehensive by any means, a partial list could look something like this:

- District Administrators
- Principals
- Assistant Principals
- Teachers
- Students
- Parents
- Mayor
- City Council
- Chamber of Commerce

- Local business owners
- Kiwanis Club
- Local universities
- Other local organizations

··· **Schedule a meeting with your stakeholder groups** ···

With a list prepared, the next step in the process is to schedule a formal meeting to discuss the *why*. These meetings should serve as conversations, not dictatorial sessions, and therefore should seek to accomplish several goals.

1. *Listen, Listen, Listen.* Use protocols to gather feedback from your stakeholders about what they want from their schools. Consider starting with the question above, *Kids learn best when...?*.

2. *Educate, Educate, Educate.* Co-construct with your stakeholders a sense that that world has changed. Think back to the technologies in Part I and the focus on the consumer experience. Ask your stakeholders how these changes should affect their schools and curriculum. In other words, build the *why* with them.

> "These meetings should serve as conversations, not dictatorial sessions, and therefore should seek to accomplish several goals."

3. *Document the data.* Use the information to inform the development of your shared vision of the modern learn-

ing environment and strategic plan.

4. *Communicate, Communicate, Communicate.* When will they hear from you again? What should they expect to hear about? Ensure that you answer these important questions. Just as before, set a clear direction to move the work forward.

··· Are they ready? ···

Naturally, some will be ready, while most will not. That's human nature, but it's not a reason to wait. Waiting may prevent the work from ever beginning. So what do you do if stakeholders are not ready? Many leaders have a "gut" feeling about the climate and culture of their organization and community. This gut is often based on past experiences, people's tolerance for new things, and how people perceive situations. While gut feelings serve as intuitive guideposts for leaders, quantifiable data provide more insights. Consider giving a short survey to gauge stakeholder readiness. The responses might surprise you, but more importantly, they will give you a roadmap for your leadership actions.

> "While gut feelings serve as intuitive guideposts for leaders, quantifiable data provide more insights."

Success Indicator #2:

Form the Digital Convergence Steering Committee

Once you establish and communicate the direction toward Digital Convergence, you must form a cross-functional team that serves as the district's Digital Convergence Steering Committee. The Steering Committee, led by you, should include executive sponsors across various disciplines (e.g., assistant superintendent, director of curriculum, director of technology, etc.). Together, the Steering Committee oversees the work of Digital Convergence, including its various stages and initiatives.

> "The Steering Committee, led by you, should include executive sponsors across various disciplines."

74

Success Indicator #3:

Develop a Theory of Action

Digital Convergence teams should consider creating a *theory of action* to use as a conversation tool. This tool can be used to facilitate stakeholders in co-constructing the vision of the modern learning environment.

A theory of action is essentially a cause and effect statement. Theory of action starters can take on many forms. Examples include:

If- then statements:

If we do this, then this will happen.

When-then statements:

When we take a particular action, then this will happen.

A theory of action will later be linked to your vision of the modern learning environment, instructional model, curriculum, ecosystem, and professional learning plan.

Success Indicator #4:

Identify and Engage Stakeholders Around the Theory of Action

Once a theory of action is created, you and the Steering Committee must set the overall effort in motion. A key starting point is to leverage the theory of action by using it with stakeholders. You should structure various activities and discussion protocols around the theory of action and engage with stakeholders in a dialogue about it. This ensures that the Steering Committee gains enough data and feedback to begin constructing the vision of the modern learning environment.

> **"Once a theory of action is created, you and the Steering Committee must set the overall effort in motion."**

Choose Your Own Adventure

As we explored in Part II, Digital Convergence occurs non-linearly, requiring work across the five drivers: leadership, instructional models, modern curriculum, digital ecosystem, and professional learning. If you want to read about the success indicators for Leadership Stage 2, refer to page 93. To learn about the next driver in Stage 1, continue reading here.

INSTRUCTIONAL MODELS
STAGE 1

76

After John F. Kennedy made his historic speech to put a man on the moon, NASA began work to ensure the vision came into fruition. Attention shifted from the outcome to the factors that would facilitate and threaten its success. Inter-disciplinary teams would oversee each of the vital aspects of the spaceflight.

Just as NASA began to operationalize Kennedy's vision, your district begins to extend the work of Leadership Stage 1 to other important areas needed for the modern learning environment. Whether redesigning pedagogical practices and assessment methods, curriculum, digital resources and infrastructure, or professional learning—these initiatives in Stage 1 largely center on developing cross-functional teams to explore solutions for the modern learning environment. As mentioned previously, your approach to these drivers can and should occur in a non-linear manner, given the systemic, interrelated nature of the effort. While this book continues by exploring instructional models, you may also begin work on the drivers of modern curriculum, digital ecosystems, and professional learning.

Instructional Models Stage 1 focuses on developing a team to explore the pedagogical practices and assessment models that effectively personalize learning and establish the modern learning environment. At this stage in the process, your district collectively recognizes the importance of the modern learning environment. It also recognizes that its current approach cannot effectively transform teaching and learning for the modern age. Your district lacks a common instructional model across its subjects, courses, and grade levels, and individual teachers or principals determine the teaching process—producing inconsistent instruction and learning outcomes across your district. Direct instruction is the prevailing pedagogy across most classrooms and often times does not accommodate diverse learning styles or needs, especially during lessons with 20 or more students. In this

> **"At this stage in the process, your district collectively recognizes the importance of the modern learning environment."**

way, traditional instruction fundamentally disrupts the transition to the modern learning environment. By developing a team to explore modern pedagogical practices and assessment models, Instructional Models Stage 1 seeks to overcome these barriers.

Success Indicator #5:
Assemble the Team

To begin work in this area, your first task is to assemble a cross-functional team to be in charge of identifying, developing, and overseeing a new instructional model for your district. Because direct instruction reduces the level of cognitive rigor in a digital environment, this representative team must work to develop a new model that leads to higher levels of rigor in the context of twenty-first-century teaching and learning. The overall objective of this team should focus on establishing a new instructional model that reflects the vision and purpose of the modern learning environment.

> **"...this team should focus on establishing a new instructional model that reflects the vision and purpose of the modern learning environment."**

The cross-functional team must have representation on the Digital Convergence Steering Committee to ensure decisions around the instructional model align with efforts across leadership, curriculum, digital ecosystem, and professional learning. The team might include varying roles—such as principals, instructional coaches, and teachers—to remove organizational silos and improve decision-making through diverse perspectives and experiences. As you work to develop this team, your district must empower one leader to oversee the larger effort, as research shows that the most effective teams operate with one representative leading the project. Your district must also clearly define objectives, resources, and priorities for this team.

Success Indicator #6:

Begin Conversations

Once the new team is assembled, it must begin exploring new instructional models that enhance teaching and learning in a digital environment. These improvements might include learner profiles, blended and personalized learning methods, and competency-based curriculum and assessments, among others. Learner profiles make personalized learning possible by identifying each student's learning preferences and style, as

> **"Learner profiles make personalized learning possible by identifying each student's learning preferences and style, as well as strengths and weaknesses."**

well as strengths and weaknesses. Blended and personalized learning methods enable students to control the pace and style of their learning, as well as the method by which they represent their learning. Competency-based assessments dictate overall progress on the education continuum and replace traditional grading systems.

Trying to integrate technology often causes problems for districts that fail to redesign their instruction for a modern environment. Digitizing traditional lesson plans and replicating poor quality online instruction are common symptoms for districts overlooking this work. Thus, the team should focus on identifying instructional models that improve cognitive rigor in a digital environment. This goes beyond just making classrooms digital or providing students choice in their learning. Instruction must continue to provide good learning outcomes to students for personalized learning to provide value.

Success Indicator #7:
Begin Conversations Around Rigor

The team should also begin conversations around developing a framework for assessing instructional rigor. As a new instructional model is introduced to your district, principals must develop new methods of assessing teachers in the modern learning environment. This ensures principals can effectively recognize pedagogy that increases cognitive rigor in a digital environment.

Developing a framework is important because it helps principals

> **"This ensures principals can effectively recognize pedagogy that increases cognitive rigor in a digital environment."**

focus less on classroom activities and more on student learning in the modern environment. The framework helps principals see that student learning is improved by cognitive rigor, rather than the number of classroom activities.

Success Indicator #8:

Begin Conversations Around Twenty-First Century Skills

In addition to rigor, the team should also begin conversations about a new framework for assessing twenty-first century skills, or preparing students for success beyond the classroom in our modern age. The framework provides discipline to and a transformation in how students are assessed, shifting the spotlight from standard assessments to those focused on competencies and mastery of concepts.

Choose Your Own Adventure

As we explored in Part II, Digital Convergence occurs non-linearly, requiring work across the five drivers: leadership, instructional models, modern curriculum, digital ecosystem, and professional learning. If you want to read about the success indicators for Instructional Models Stage 2, refer to page 98. To learn about the next driver in Stage 1, continue reading here.

MODERN CURRICULUM
STAGE 1

82

Just as traditional instruction prevents modern learning from taking place, so too does traditional curriculum. Except for date of birth, traditional curriculum treats students as equal entities in the education continuum—ignoring the personal learning styles and needs that determine student outcomes. In this way, traditional curriculum lacks the flexibility to tailor the learning experience to the individual student. Blended unit plans opti-

> "Blended unit plans optimize curriculum for the modern learning environment by providing personalized, individualized learning experiences that focus on competency and mastery-based learning."

mize curriculum for the modern learning environment by providing personalized, individualized learning experiences that focus on competency and mastery-based learning. As your district explores pedagogical practices and assessment methods that are effective in the modern age, it also begins to explore curriculum that produces the competencies to compete in the twenty-first century. At this stage, your district is beginning to explore a common blended unit plan across all subjects, courses, and grade levels. The blended unit plan is still in the development phase; therefore, individual teachers cannot incorporate it into teaching and learning yet.

Success Indicator #9:

Explore a Common Blended Unit Plan

Blended unit plans pair personalized and individualized online learning with face-to-face teaching and learning. The effort to develop curriculum that transforms teaching and learning for the modern environment begins when your district explores a common blended unit plan. This plan should transcend all subjects, courses, and grade levels.

> "The effort to develop curriculum that transforms teaching and learning for the modern environment begins when your district explores a common blended unit plan."

─────── **Choose Your Own Adventure** ───────

As we explored in Part II, Digital Convergence occurs non-linearly, requiring work across the five drivers: leadership, instructional models, modern curriculum, digital ecosystem, and professional learning. If you want to read about the success indicators for Modern Curriculum Stage 2, refer to page 102. To learn about the next driver in Stage 1, continue reading here.

DIGITAL ECOSYSTEM
STAGE 1

84

As NASA prepared for its mission to the moon, a critical focus was ensuring that the spaceship could effectively bring astronauts to and from the moon. This meant countless hours testing, working out kinks, and ensuring that the spaceship properly functioned as a unified system of gadgets, instruments, and technology. In the journey toward Digital Convergence, this is analogous to ensuring that digital resources integrate, interconnect, and function seamlessly as a unified network.

"...this is analogous to ensuring that digital resources integrate, interconnect, and function seamlessly as a unified network."

Just as your district formed teams for your important Stage 1 leadership and instructional model activities, you also begin assembling a cross-functional team to oversee and support your digital ecosystem. As you begin work in this stage, your district's digital resources remain disconnected and disorganized, with no plan or systematic process for tracking, integrating, coordinating, or supporting digital devices and content. The use of digital tools varies across the district and differs from teacher to teacher. The cross-functional team is charged with overseeing all digital resources to support the modern learning environment now and in the future.

Success Indicator #10:
Assemble the Team

To begin work creating a digital ecosystem, your first task is to assemble another cross-functional team charged with overseeing its development and ongoing support. Since digital resources are often disparate and untracked, this team focuses on creating a net-

> **"...a critical step is to appoint a leader to oversee the work of the digital ecosystem."**

work that integrates, interconnects, and supports all resources to promote access and a seamless user experience.

Like the team for the new instructional model, this group

should also sit on the Digital Convergence Steering Committee to ensure decisions align with other initiatives. It should include a diverse set of stakeholders that incorporates school-based leaders, educators, and IT staff. As you form the team, a critical step is to appoint a leader to oversee the work of the digital ecosystem. Also important is establishing the team's objectives, resources, and priorities.

The size of your district is an important consideration when assembling and designing your digital ecosystem team. For large districts, an effective model is to design the team in tiers. The top tier consists of executive sponsors who oversee the entire ecosystem, followed by a steering committee of executive sponsors and subject matter experts. Below the steering committee, the team should comprise workgroups assigned to each of the various subsystems and include one executive sponsor, multiple subject matter experts, and other personnel charged with making decisions. Members of the subunit should sit on the digital ecosystem steering committee to ensure full representation and alignment. Smaller districts benefit from an abbreviated team structure.

Success Indicator #11:
Begin Conversations

When the new team is formed, it should begin conversations around the digital ecosystem, with a focus on its purpose, users, systems, subsystems, and functions. Eventually, the team should develop a vision and mission for the digital ecosystem that aligns with the district's overall vision. It should also identify each user group and its level of access, as well as identify the vital systems, subsystems, and respective functions to begin understanding how the ecosystem operates.

> "Establishing a vision for the digital ecosystem helps overcome competing priorities and expectations..."

Establishing a vision for the digital ecosystem helps overcome competing priorities and expectations for the ecosystem. Without a collective vision, stakeholders often disagree and miscommunicate the purpose, design, and function of the digital ecosystem. A good practice for the team is to start their conversations by documenting, agreeing on, and communicating the vision and purpose for the ecosystem. This ensures that the team has a framework to guide their decision-making process as the ecosystem is developed and supported in the future.

The team must also begin discussing how the ecosystem will support and align with the district's new instructional model.

Choose Your Own Adventure

As we explored in Part II, Digital Convergence occurs non-linearly, requiring work across the five drivers: leadership, instructional models, modern curriculum, digital ecosystem, and professional learning. If you want to read about the success indicators for Digital Ecosystem Stage 2, refer to page 105. To learn about the next driver in Stage 1, continue reading here.

PROFESSIONAL LEARNING
STAGE 1

88

The success of NASA's mission to the moon depended on, among other things, astronauts' training. Think of everything astronauts had to learn to safely land—from operating the spaceship, to understanding the dangers and constraints of space, to even performing activities of daily living in zero gravity. Even with Kennedy's directive, NASA's vision, and the capability of the spaceship, the mission would have invariably failed if this important factor was overlooked.

> "The final ingredient needed for the modern learning environment is professional learning."

The final ingredient needed for the modern learning environment is professional learning. Professional learning determines our teachers' ability to use technology in ways that facilitate personalized learning. This goes far beyond training them how to operate a new device or access digital content; instead, it gives them the knowledge, skills, and abilities to optimize student outcomes through technology within the context of the new instructional model, modern curriculum, and digital ecosystem.

As you approach this phase of work, your district's current professional learning opportunities are isolated, left to chance or the interest of individual teachers or administrators, and disconnected from instructional design and teaching strategies. Professional learning opportunities may be relegated to the start or end of the school year, minimizing teachers' and staff's ability to retain learning. It may also occur sporadically, leaving teachers and stakeholders unprepared to perform their role effectively. Additionally, it might focus on limited information, such as instructing teachers on the features and functions of new technology without addressing the strategies and teaching methods that drive its effective

> **"Your natural starting point at this stage is to assemble a cross-functional team to oversee and support professional learning programs and activities."**

use in a classroom setting. Your natural starting point at this stage is to assemble a cross-functional team to oversee and support professional learning programs and activities.

Success Indicator #12:
Assemble the Team

Just as you assembled a team for instructional models and digital ecosystem, you must also establish a cross-functional team to oversee professional learning. This team should also serve on the Digital Convergence Steering Committee to ensure its decisions align with all other projects and initiatives. The team should include diverse stakeholders, such as principals, IT staff, instructional coaches, curriculum writers, and teachers. As the leader, you should appoint one representative to oversee all professional learning and empower the team to make decisions. You should also clearly establish the team's objectives, resources, and priorities.

> **"This team should also serve on the Digital Convergence Steering Committee to ensure its decisions align with all other projects and initiatives."**

Choose Your Own Adventure

As we explored in Part II, Digital Convergence occurs non-linearly, requiring work across the five drivers: leadership, instructional models, modern curriculum, digital ecosystem, and professional learning. If you want to read about the success indicators for Professional Learning Stage 2, refer to page 110. To learn about Leadership Stage 2, continue reading here.

STAGE 2

LEADERSHIP
STAGE 2

In Stage 1, our efforts largely centered on developing the foundation from which to begin our journey toward Digital Convergence. We set the direction, engaged stakeholders, and formed teams to explore instructional models, curriculum, digital resources, and professional learning. Stage 2

> **"Stage 2 Leadership entails creating awareness of the district's new vision for the modern learning environment, as well as branding and aligning the overall initiative."**

93

continues to build on this progress by solidifying the new direction of the district. For instance, Stage 2 Leadership entails creating awareness of the district's new vision for the modern learning environment, as well as branding and aligning the overall initiative. The other Stage 2 drivers deal with defining the district's new instructional model, blended unit plan, digital ecosystem and its nested elements, and professional learning plan and approach.

While Stage 1 focuses on developing the structures and processes to develop the modern learning environment, Stage 2 is where the real work begins.

You set the direction for your district in terms of developing a personalized learning experience for students. You also invited stakeholders into the process to collectively develop the vision for the modern learning environment. In Stage 2, your focus shifts from preparing the district to generating awareness of its new focus. This is the natural next step to lead the work of the other drivers in Stage 2. As the leader of your district, you must continue to promote the effort by ensuring that stakeholders remain aware, engaged, and aligned. You must also ensure that the effort remains a priority amid competing initiatives that threaten to distract you. A critical focus during this stage is broadcasting the new vision to stakeholders in a way that is exciting and memorable. It also entails aligning the effort with other strategic initiatives. At this stage of work, early adopters and enthusiastic individuals drive most conversations around the modern learning environment and act as champions of the new vision.

> "As the leader of your district, you must continue to promote the effort by ensuring that stakeholders remain aware, engaged, and aligned."

94

Success Indicator #13:
Communicate the Vision

You have set the direction for your district and engaged stakeholders to develop the vision and mission of the modern learning environment. You are now ready to inform, engage, and empower stakeholders on the journey toward Digital Convergence. An important step in this ongoing process is to communicate the successful development of the district's vision for the modern learning environment.

> **"There are multiple ways to promote awareness of the newly developed vision."**

There are multiple ways to promote awareness of the newly developed vision. Presentations, forums, emails, memos, and other forms of communication all serve as viable options for communicating the vision. I have found that promoting awareness is best achieved when you formally present the vision of the modern learning environment to stakeholders. Your presentation should not only introduce the vision, but also recount the collective process used to create it. Important to your speech is emphasizing the sense of urgency and responsibility to engage in the work to transform teaching and learning for the modern age.

Success Indicator #14:
Share the Vision Deck

After you present your district's vision of the modern learning environment, another step is to share it with stakeholders as a tangible asset that they can refer to in the future as your district continues its journey toward Digital Convergence.

Success Indicator #15:
Establish a Shared Vocabulary

Developing a common language for Digital Convergence is vital to the successful transition to modern learning environments. Without a common vocabulary, stakeholders misinterpret and misunderstand messages, leading to confusion, resistance, inefficiency, and other problems. To facilitate meaningful and productive conversations, you must develop a common vocabulary for the barriers, solutions, and benefits of the modern learning environment. This ensures your district can optimize the efficiency and effectiveness of the collective effort.

"Without a common vocabulary, stakeholders misinterpret and misunderstand messages, leading to confusion, resistance, inefficiency, and other problems."

To create a common vocabulary, work with the Digital Convergence Steering Committee to identify and define key terms that pertain to the modern learning environment. These include the concept of Digital Convergence, its drivers, as well as the barriers to twenty-first-century teaching and learning, such as single-point solutions.

Success Indicator #16:
Establish a Brand

The work of Digital Convergence is an ongoing priority for your district. To promote awareness of and engagement in the overall effort, and to increase the visibility and transparency of the initiative, your district should develop a brand for Digital Convergence. Complete with a name and logo, this brand should speak to your district's overall vision and serve as a memorable symbol that motivates and inspires stakeholders.

97

Success Indicator #17:
Align the Work of Digital Convergence to Your Strategic Plan

To ensure that the work of Digital Convergence remains a priority for your district, you must align it to your district's strategic plan. This guarantees that the work of Digital Convergence remains front-of-mind and does

"This guarantees that the work of Digital Convergence remains front-of-mind and does not compete with other important initiatives."

not compete with other important initiatives. It also increases your district's chances for success in the transition to modern learning environments.

Choose Your Own Adventure

As we explored in Part II, Digital Convergence occurs non-linearly, requiring work across the five drivers: leadership, instructional models, modern curriculum, digital ecosystem, and professional learning. If you want to read about the success indicators for Leadership Stage 3, refer to page 117. To learn about the next driver in Stage 2, continue reading here.

98

INSTRUCTIONAL MODELS
STAGE 2

In his book *From Good to Great*, author Jim Collins introduced the concept of the Flywheel Effect—a metaphor to describe how companies have achieved remarkable results over time. The Flywheel Effect posits that organizations do not achieve outstanding results overnight. Instead, they realize achievements slowly over time by making good choices that build positive momentum (Collins 2001, 164-169).

In the context of developing the modern learning environment, the work of Instructional Models Stage 2 represents one of the many actions needed to build the momentum of the flywheel. By now, the team assigned to this important area of work has explored instructional models that are effective in a digital environment. The team's focus shifts from exploration to definition: it seeks to solidify the new instructional model as well as the frameworks for assessing cognitive rigor and twenty-first-century skills. These actions build momentum as your district begins to develop model blended units that are aligned to the instructional model. The new instructional model promotes personalization, blended learning, digital content, and media integration.

> "The team's focus shifts from exploration to definition: it seeks to solidify the new instructional model as well as the frameworks for assessing cognitive rigor and twenty-first-century skills."

Success Indicator #18:
Define the New Instructional Model

After exploring pedagogical and assessment practices, the team overseeing this area of work must begin to define the district's new instructional model. The team should define the model in a manner that is intelligible and easy for principals, teachers, and other stakeholders to understand. This includes developing standards for the instructional model, as well as a graphic model for visual representation. Helping teachers and principals see how the instructional model fits into the creation of the modern learning environment increases their overall engagement and ownership of the transition. The professional learning team should define the new instructional model in terms of rigor and relevance.

> **"Helping teachers and principals see how the instructional model fits into the creation of the modern learning environment increases their overall engagement and ownership of the transition."**

100

Success Indicator #19:
Finalize Framework for Assessing Rigor

To ensure principals can effectively evaluate teachers on instructional rounds, the team should also develop and finalize an agreed-upon evaluation framework. The framework should be intelligible to principals and teachers, and clearly identify effective and ineffective teaching practices in the modern learning environment. Like the overall instructional model, representing the framework visually helps ensure principals and teachers effectively understand it.

Success Indicator #20:

Finalize Framework for Assessing Twenty-First-Century Skills

Because the new instructional model is replacing existing assessment methods, the team should also define a new framework for assessing twenty-first-century skills. This ensures that students are assessed based on their competencies and mastery of concepts, rather than their ability to perform on standard assessments. The assessment framework serves to establish accountability even as more flexible learning paths are introduced and students begin to learn at their own pace. Again, the instructional model team should develop a graphical representation of this framework to facilitate teacher comprehension and understanding.

When developing the competencies that each student should obtain upon graduation, your district should review national and state standards, such as Common Core State Standards for ELA, Next Generation Science Standards, and C3 Framework for Social Studies. Together with your teachers, your district should analyze these standards to create competencies that hold students accountable for their learning and produce

> **"When developing the competencies that each student should obtain upon graduation, your district should review national and state standards..."**

graduates who are college- and career-ready.

In this phase, your instructional model team should work to develop assessments that provide students multiple means of representing their learning. Whether through kinesthetic, visual, or verbal means, students should receive the opportunity to demonstrate their learning according to their preferences and strengths.

Choose Your Own Adventure

As we explored in Part II, Digital Convergence occurs non-linearly, requiring work across the five drivers: leadership, instructional models, modern curriculum, digital ecosystem, and professional learning. If you want to read about the success indicators for Instructional Models Stage 3, refer to page 123. To learn about the next driver in Stage 2, continue reading here.

MODERN CURRICULUM
STAGE 2

With the new instructional model defined, your district is ready to develop curriculum that facilitates personalized learning in the modern learning environment. While Stage 1 focused on exploring a common blended unit plan, Stage 2 entails assessing digital content, finalizing the blended unit plan, and developing model digital/blended units. These model units should be aligned with the instructional model and made available inside your digital ecosystem.

Success Indicator #21:
Assess Digital Content

As your district begins developing a common blended unit plan, it must also identify all its digital content, including purchased content and any free content teachers may be using. By inventorying these resources, your district can better understand how digital content is currently being used and develop a plan for developing curriculum that is aligned with your instructional framework.

103

Success Indicator #22:
Finalize Common Blended Unit Plan

Your district should develop a common blended unit plan that is aligned with the new instructional model across all subjects, courses, and grade levels. The blended unit plan includes common protocols for how your

"The blended unit plan includes common protocols for how your district builds its curriculum in a digital environment."

district builds its curriculum in a digital environment. This ensures that curriculum is personalized and individualized to students.

Success Indicator #23:
Develop Model Blended Lessons

Your district should also work to develop model lessons that align with the blended unit plan and the new instructional model. These model lessons serve as a resource to educators and other stakeholders and should be accessible via your digital ecosystem.

Choose Your Own Adventure

As we explored in Part II, Digital Convergence occurs non-linearly, requiring work across the five drivers: leadership, instructional models, modern curriculum, digital ecosystem, and professional learning. If you want to read about the success indicators for Modern Curriculum Stage 3, refer to page 124. To learn about the next driver in Stage 2, continue reading here.

DIGITAL ECOSYSTEM
STAGE 2

Using the analogy of the flywheel, your district is gaining momentum in the transition toward modern learning environments. You've communicated the vision of the modern learning environment to stakeholders, branded the initiative, and developed a shared vocabulary to support long-term awareness and engagement. The teams assigned to the instructional model and curriculum are busy finalizing models to support teaching and learning on a broad scale. Now, the digital ecosystem team turns its focus from exploring the possibilities of the ecosystem to defining, assembling, and assessing its critical components. In terms of defining the ecosystem, the team collaborates to identify the clear purpose of the ecosystem, as well as its various user groups. It then seeks to identify the major systems and subsystems that comprise the network. In terms of assembling, the team makes its first procurement decision by acquiring a next generation learning management system (LMS)—a resource that serves an integral purpose to the ecosystem, including providing access to digital content,

"...the team makes its first procurement decision by acquiring a next generation learning management system (LMS)..."

tracking progress, etc. Lastly, the team assesses the district's digital resources to inform its subsequent work.

Success Indicator #24:
Define Purpose and Users

Important to the development of your digital ecosystem is understanding its purpose and users. The digital ecosystem team should collaborate to define both components. The purpose should align to the overall vision of the modern learning environment, while users should comprise a list of each stakeholder group and its level of access.

Defining the purpose and user groups of your ecosystem is a vital step in the process. Your ecosystem should serve users by providing them access when and where they need it; ensuring the privacy and security of their data; and offering a seamless, optimal user experience as they interact with resources. Because users are central to the ecosystem, it must reflect their needs, values, and preferences now and in the future.

> **"Defining the purpose and user groups of your ecosystem is a vital step in the process."**

106

Success Indicator #25:

Define Systems, Subsystems, and Functions

Another indicator of success occurs when the team defines the systems, subsystems, and functions of the digital ecosystem. The team identifies the components of the ecosystem and how they interrelate. Through this definition, stakeholders gain a clear understanding of the ecosystem and its constituents.

"Through this definition, stakeholders gain a clear understanding of the ecosystem and its constituents."

To understand the components of the ecosystem, the team meets with executive sponsors, subject matter experts, or other personnel to gather the functionality and content requirements for the systems and subsystems. Then, the team can begin to develop a supportive infrastructure that facilitates interoperability, which is vital to providing a seamless user experience.

Success Indicator #26:

Procure a Learning Management System

The learning management system (LMS) serves a vital purpose in the digital ecosystem. The LMS houses your digital educational content, tracks proficiency and completion, and manages reporting and administration, as well as other key functions. Given its importance, your district achieves another success indicator when it procures an LMS for its digital ecosystem. The LMS comprises one of many integral systems that make up your ecosystem and therefore should be integrated.

> "One tendency for districts is to treat the LMS as the digital ecosystem. Known as the portal philosophy, this type of LMS serves as a single-point solution..."

One tendency for districts is to treat the LMS as the digital ecosystem. Known as the portal philosophy, this type of LMS serves as a single-point solution that impedes rather than facilitates the ultimate goal of personalized learning for students.

Success Indicator #27:

Extend the Digital Convergence Brand

Your district must extend your brand of the modern learning environment to the digital ecosystem. This includes developing a name for the ecosystem, a medium for ongoing communication with stakeholders, and visuals to represent the conceptual design of the ecosystem. The brand serves to promote awareness, engagement, and understanding of the ecosystem.

It is important that your digital ecosystem remain

consistent across all materials, resources, and curriculum. Often these components provide users with an inconsistent experience across content areas and grade levels. Branding the ecosystem and its connected elements unifies the look and feel of digital

> **"Branding the ecosystem and its connected elements unifies the look and feel of digital resources..."**

resources to provide a uniform experience across user groups, content areas, and grade levels.

Success Indicator #28:
Assess Digital Tools

The digital ecosystem team must conduct a full-scale assessment of your district's digital tools, including purchased and high-access free resources. Conducting this assessment ensures that the team can identify all resources currently in use by the district and

> **"Conducting this assessment ensures that the team can identify all resources currently in use..."**

begin integrating these resources within the context of the ecosystem's defined purpose, users, and components.

Choose Your Own Adventure

As we explored in Part II, Digital Convergence occurs non-linearly, requiring work across the five drivers: leadership, instructional models, modern curriculum, digital ecosystem, and professional learning. If you want to read about the success indicators for Digital Ecosystem Stage 3, refer to page 126. To learn about the next driver in Stage 2, continue reading here.

PROFESSIONAL LEARNING
STAGE 2

As you work across the drivers in Stage 2, your professional learning team focuses on developing the infrastructure and support systems to effectively roll out scaled professional learning. While Stage 1 of professional learning focused on assembling the team in charge of professional learning, Stage 2 transitions to develop the plan, processes, and personnel to ensure teachers, staff, and other stakeholders gain the education they need to excel in the modern learning environment. In this phase of work, the team develops a professional learning plan, complete with the various programs, timelines, and stakeholder groups. It also develops an implementation model to ensure professional learning programs are scalable and replicable. The team then focuses on preparing instructional coaches, who serve as at-the-elbow, ongoing support for teachers and other stakeholders. Professional learning begins during this stage as the first group of teachers are grouped into cohorts, where the instructional coaches introduce the district's new approach to professional learning.

> "The team then focuses on preparing instructional coaches, who serve as at-the-elbow, ongoing support for teachers and other stakeholders."

Success Indicator #29:
Identify Implementation Model

111

Because of the size and scope of the effort, your professional learning team should develop an implementation model. This implementation model should outline the necessary resources, timelines, and milestones to successfully implement professional learning to your teachers, school-based leaders, and other stakeholders. The implementation model serves as a framework to ensure the team prepares for each professional learning program. It also serves to make the process more efficient, effective, and repeatable as professional learning is rolled out across multiple cohorts and stakeholder groups.

Success Indicator #30:

Identify Instructional Coaches

Important to professional learning is identifying and selecting instructional coaches to provide at-the-elbow support for professional learning programs. The professional learning team should identify internal coaches to support Digital Convergence consistent with your district's implementation model.

> **"In large and even small districts, instructional coaches act as 'feet on the ground.'"**

In large and even small districts, instructional coaches act as "feet on the ground." These individuals remove the silos that naturally exist in our school systems by offering support across departments. Districts that have been successful in this area have developed coaches to serve as ambassadors and support personnel for their respective buildings or departments.

Success Indicator #31:

Develop a Professional Learning Plan

Another indicator of success occurs when the cross-functional team develops a professional learning plan. This plan must be consistent with the district's overall implementation model and include corresponding timelines and milestones

112

for success. This plan should serve to provide ongoing professional learning through multiple mediums, including online and remote learning.

Other areas of focus include providing education that spans both technology and content, as well as developing effective employee-onboarding programs to bring new hires up to speed.

> "Other areas of focus include providing education that spans both technology and content, as well as developing effective employee-onboarding programs to bring new hires up to speed."

speed. The professional learning plan should focus on providing professional learning programs that optimize access, consistency, relevancy, and replicability.

Success Indicator #32:
Prepare Coaches

After identifying your district's instructional coaches, the professional learning team demonstrates another success indicator when it prepares a critical mass of coaches to support the initial cohort launch. The team should provide the coaches with the needed knowledge, materials, and time to successfully deliver professional learning to this group of teachers.

Success Indicator #33:

Select Teachers for Cohorts

After preparing the instructional coaches, the cross-functional team should begin selecting and grouping teachers into professional learning cohorts consistent with your district's implementation model.

Success Indicator #34:

Kick Off Cohorts

The next success indicator occurs when instructional coaches kick off their teacher cohorts with a face-to-face session to set expectations, build awareness of tools and resources, and generate excitement for the journey ahead. This session should introduce teachers to the district's overall vision of the modern learning environment, the new instructional model, blended unit plan and model lessons, and digital ecosystem.

"This session should introduce teachers to the district's overall vision of the modern learning environment, the new instructional model, blended unit plan and model lessons, and digital ecosystem."

Choose Your Own Adventure

As we explored in Part II, Digital Convergence occurs non-linearly, requiring work across the five drivers: leadership, instructional models, modern curriculum, digital ecosystem, and professional learning. If you want to read about the success indicators for Professional Learning Stage 3, refer to page 129. To learn about Leadership Stage 3, continue reading here.

STAGE 3

LEADERSHIP
STAGE 3

Entering Stage 3, your district's momentum toward the modern learning environment continues to build. By now, you've made considerable progress in Stage 1 and 2 that is worth recognizing. In Leadership Stage 3, you will highlight the achievements your district is making across the five drivers of Digital Convergence. Your focus will also shift from the high-level work of establishing a vision to the tactical efforts of extending the reach of your leadership. This will include educating school-based leaders; developing vehicles for long-term, ongoing communication; and capturing metrics to gauge progress. Following their training, school-based leaders will be prepared to serve as active participants in promoting and championing the vision, clearly articulate the difference between first- and second-order change, and facilitate "culture conversations" at their schools. At this point, substantial input from all teachers has been

117

> **"Your focus will also shift from the high-level work of establishing a vision to the tactical efforts of extending the reach of your leadership."**

part of the vision development process, and your district will begin to actively promote the Digital Convergence brand through multiple distribution channels.

Success Indicator #35:

Communicate Key Wins and Next Steps

In Stage 3 Leadership, your responsibility to generate awareness of Digital Convergence transitions from introducing Digital Convergence to highlighting the progress and achievements your district is making. Another success indicator occurs when you communicate key wins in Digital Convergence to all stakeholders.

> "Another success indicator occurs when you communicate key wins in Digital Convergence to all stakeholders."

These key wins should cover the indicators of success achieved in Stage 1 and Stage 2 of Digital Convergence. The development of a new instructional model, the creation of a blended unit plan, the development of a brand for the digital ecosystem, the creation of professional learning cohorts, etc.—all represent key accomplishments to include in your message. In addition to recognizing your district's progress, you must also set the path forward by outlining the next action items in the journey. This means discussing each of the success indicators contained in Stage 3 of the Digital Convergence Framework.

118

Success Indicator #36:

Train School-Based Leaders

Principals and other school-based leaders must understand how to effectively manage the transition for their school and its stakeholders. This requires school-based leaders to understand the change management process. Your district experiences an indicator of success when it trains all school-based leaders on leading change through change management theory and first- and second-order change. Through these efforts, your school-based leaders can effectively mitigate resistance, as well as the emotional and psychological impact of the transition.

119

The work of William Bridges in *Managing Transitions* serves as a vital resource for this effort. As a leader, your task is to help school-based leaders understand the emotions involved with the shift toward modern learning environments. Your efforts should focus on helping school-based leaders feel prepared to address the emotions of stakeholders

"Through these efforts, your school-based leaders can effectively mitigate resistance, as well as the emotional and psychological impact of the transition."

in their schools. In addition to training these leaders on the transformation of instruction and curriculum, you must also cover the transition these leaders must make in their leadership practices.

Success Indicator #37:
Create Plans for Culture Conversations

School-based leaders must address the need to transition to modern learning environments with their stakeholders. Another success indicator occurs when your district creates school-based plans to facilitate "culture conversations," which explore the culture of the modern learning environment and articulate the need to transform teaching and learning for the twenty-first century. This plan should include the key messages to educate stakeholders, as well as a plan to address questions and concerns. It should also frame the conversations in the context of the district's overall vision of the modern learning environment.

> "This plan should include the key messages to educate stakeholders, as well as a plan to address questions and concerns."

Success Indicator #38:
School-Based Leaders Facilitate Culture Conversations

Once the plan is created, another success indicator occurs when school-based leaders operationalize it and begin facilitating the culture conversations. The conversations should focus on setting direction; creating a sense of urgency and engagement in the work; as well as mitigating anxiety, fears, and resistance to the change. Stakeholders should leave the sessions educated on and prepared to make the transition.

> **"The conversations should focus on setting direction; creating a sense of urgency and engagement in the work; as well as mitigating anxiety, fears, and resistance to the change."**

Success Indicator #39:
Develop Plans to Communicate the Work of Digital Convergence

Your district achieves another success indicator when it develops a plan to regularly communicate the work of Digital Convergence. This plan should identify the various media outlets to reach internal and external stakeholders, including parents and community members. The plan should also outline the strategic and tactical information to ensure regular communication.

Success Indicator #40:
Establish Metrics and Formalize a Reflection Process

Understanding your district's progress toward Digital Convergence is vital to your overall success. To gauge your progress across the five drivers of Digital Convergence, you must identify and establish metrics that accurately reflect advancements toward modern learning environments. You must define metrics for each driver of Digital Convergence. Because work across the five drivers of Digital Convergence should remain relatively uniform, these metrics enable you to refocus and reprioritize your efforts and resources as needed.

122

The work across the first three stages of the Digital Convergence Framework is iterative and non-linear. As the leader of your district, it's vitally important for you to provide stakeholders an opportunity to reflect on the district's progress to date. Up until Leadership Stage 3, this occurs during informal meetings and gatherings between you and stakeholders. As you enter Stage 3, however, formalizing this reflection process becomes vitally important to document and synthesize the successes and missed opportunities of the overall effort. The formal reflection process serves as a routine

> "...you must identify and establish metrics that accurately reflect advancements toward modern learning environments."

health check that guides and refines the work of your district over time, maintains alignment, and sustains engagement by giving stakeholders a platform for voicing feedback. Focus groups, interviews, and other feedback mechanisms are some useful ways to collect quantitative and qualitative data needed for synthesis. After analyzing the data, the formal reflection process then entails developing and reporting recommendations to refine the work of Digital Convergence for the future.

INSTRUCTIONAL MODELS
STAGE 3

As you communicate key wins for the district and prepare school-based leaders to manage the transition, your instructional model team begins to solicit feedback from instructional staff regarding the newly defined instructional model. In this way, the focus during this stage transitions from defining the pedagogical practices and assessment methods that are effective in a digital environment, to gathering feedback and making refinements as appropriate. This process is iterative. It not only validates the effectiveness

> "It not only validates the effectiveness for the instructional model, but it also fosters additional engagement and ownership of the model..."

for the instructional model, but it also fosters additional engagement and ownership of the model among participating stakeholders. Like Leadership Stage 3, this serves to further extend the reach of the work occurring in this driver.

Success Indicator #41:
Engage Additional Instructional Staff

Your district achieves another success indicator when the professional learning team identifies and engages additional instructional staff in providing feedback around the newly defined instructional model. The instructional staff should comprise a group of teachers who are piloting the new pedagogical practices and assessment methods, as well as principals evaluating these teachers on instructional rounds.

MODERN CURRICULUM
STAGE 3

Momentum continues to build as the district begins curriculum work in Stage 3 of Digital Convergence. By now, your district has developed model blended lessons that provide teachers a template for developing curriculum in the modern learning environment. As you enter this stage, your district develops blended units, makes them available in your digital ecosystem, and begins to develop plans to address gaps in digital content across subjects, courses, and grade levels.

Success Indicator #42:
Develop Model Blended Units

Your district demonstrates another success indicator when model blended units have been developed. Part of this success indicator includes making sure educators and staff can access the blended units via your digital ecosystem. These blended units must be aligned to the new instructional model.

Success Indicator #43:
Identify Gaps in Digital Content

In Stage 2 of modern curriculum, your district identified all digital content in use, including purchased and free content. Your next task is to use this information to identify any gaps across all subjects, courses, and grade levels. For each gap, your district should develop a plan to address it.

> **"Your next task is to use this information to identify any gaps across all subjects, courses, and grade levels."**

DIGITAL ECOSYSTEM
STAGE 3

In Stage 2, your digital ecosystem team focused mostly on defining the critical components of the network. In Stage 3, the focus transitions to establishing rhythm and coordination among the members of the team to ensure that the digital ecosystem is supported and sustained for the future. The digital ecosystem team establishes a regular cadence to work on integration needs, monitor progress, and review milestones continuously. The team's focus also shifts to establishing a hierarchical rollout plan of the ecosystem to user groups.

> "The digital ecosystem team establishes a regular cadence to work on integration needs, monitor progress, and review milestones continuously."

126

Success Indicator #44:
Establish a Cadence

The need to sustain, support, and evaluate the digital ecosystem is ongoing. Your district demonstrates an indicator of success when the digital ecosystem team establishes a regular cadence for meeting and collaborating as it continuously reviews integration needs, progress monitoring, and milestones.

This regular cadence allows the team to effectively oversee the digital ecosystem and anticipate issues that may impact integration, impede access, or diminish the user experience. It also promotes the integrity of the digital ecosystem as your district procures more digital resources.

> **"It also promotes the integrity of the digital ecosystem as your district procures more digital resources."**

Establishing a cadence also entails beginning to develop processes and policies for working with vendors. The team should seek to partner with vendors that share the mission, vision, and purpose of your ecosystem, and can contribute to its efficiency and effectiveness. The process should use several methods to qualify vendors, such as surveys, interviews, demonstrations, and testing in your environment. While this process slows procurement, it eliminates downstream problems such as frustration from functional or integration-related issues.

Success Indicator #45:
Establish the Go-Live Date

Planning is essential to the implementation and adoption of the digital ecosystem. To ensure success in these areas, the digital ecosystem team should define a hierarchical rollout to stakeholder groups and set go-live dates for internal testing and tiered access. The team should plan for an adequate period of testing to ensure the ecosystem operates effectively and efficiently before providing access. This level of planning minimizes unforeseen problems and bottlenecks, promoting success.

> **"Planning is essential to the implementation and adoption of the digital ecosystem."**

As your team sets the go-live schedule, an important and often overlooked activity is to educate help desk and support staff on the digital ecosystem. These stakeholders provide crucial support to users during and after go-live, and therefore must be brought up to speed well in advance of the rollout.

After the ecosystem is live, the team must shift to support the refinement and evolution of the ecosystem. One important task is to develop a system with timelines for refinements to take place. Making changes to the digital ecosystem disrupts the environment, such as user access and interaction. This requires the digital ecosystem team to think strategically about how and when to make enhancements to the ecosystem without interrupting access. Districts that have demonstrated success in this area have analyzed the habits of users and focused enhancements on parts of the system at a time.

PROFESSIONAL LEARNING
STAGE 3

In Stage 2, the professional learning team created the structures and support systems to develop, deploy, monitor, and sustain professional learning for all user groups. While Stage 2 focused on preparation, Stage 3 centers on deployment. All professional learning programs

"All professional learning programs are assessed and monitored for effectiveness based on multiple data points..."

grams are assessed and monitored for effectiveness based on multiple data points, and the professional learning teams meet success indicators as they help stakeholders achieve proficiency in the modern learning environment for their respective roles.

Success Indicator #46:

Deploy and Monitor School-Based Leadership Professional Learning

As mentioned previously, school-based leadership must understand how to effectively transition their populations to modern learning environments. Your district demonstrates a success indicator when it provides school-based leadership with professional learning. It also demonstrates clear

129

evidence that the professional learning team is continuously monitoring the effectiveness of the program based on multiple data points.

Success Indicator #47:
Develop Professional Learning Plans

Important to the success of professional learning are long-term plans to educate teachers on Digital Convergence. Your district demonstrates a success indicator when professional learning plans are developed for new teacher induction and include a pathway for all new teachers to be fluent in Digital Convergence within the first three years of their employment.

130

Professional learning offers the opportunity to educate stakeholders on how to perform effectively in the context of their role in the modern learning environment. It also provides the ability to reinforce the benefits of personalized learning by exposing teachers, principals, and staff to this approach from the perspective of a student. For this reason, professional learning programs should be designed through the same lens as student learning. Multiple learn-

> **"Professional learning offers the opportunity to educate stakeholders on how to perform effectively in the context of their role in the modern learning environment."**

ing choices and paths; multiple means of representation; competency- and mastery-based assessments; improved access, consistency, etc.—all represent important criteria to consider when designing and planning professional learning.

Success Indicator #48:
Deploy and Monitor Coaches

After selecting and training instructional coaches, the professional learning team should deploy them to provide ongoing support to teachers. Also important is ensuring that the professional learning team continuously monitors the effectiveness of instructional coach support based on multiple data points.

131

Success Indicator #49:
Deploy and Monitor Teacher Cohort Professional Learning

With teachers grouped into cohorts, the professional learning team should deploy their education. It should also continuously monitor the effectiveness of their professional learning based on multiple data points.

Success Indicator #50-54:

Achieve Literacy and Fluency

The goal of your professional learning programs is to establish literacy, fluency, and mastery of content areas. While literacy represents *the ability to articulate knowledge in the context of one's job,* fluency represents *the ability to perform a task with ease.* Your professional learning team demonstrates multiple success indicators when stakeholder groups achieve levels of literacy and fluency in their respective roles. This level of competency is called proficiency. There are several success indicators that fall into this category.

> "While literacy represents *the ability to articulate knowledge in the context of one's job,* fluency represents *the ability to perform a task with ease.*"

- *Success Indicator #50: A critical mass of school-based leadership achieves literacy in change management practices.*
- *Success Indicator #51: A critical mass of instructional coaches achieves literacy in the role of architect.*
- *Success Indicator #52: A critical mass of instructional coaches achieves fluency in the role of architect.*
- *Success Indicator #53: 10 percent of teachers achieve literacy in the role of architect.*
- *Success Indicator #54: 10 percent of teachers achieve fluency in the role of architect.*

132

Success Indicator #55:

Begin Conversations about Student Outcome Metrics

Your district demonstrates advancement toward Digital Convergence when it begins discussions about student outcome metrics that go beyond quantitative state assessments.

• • •

As mentioned before, the first three stages of Digital Convergence represent the early and emerging progress of districts transitioning to a modern learning environment. While the Digital Convergence Framework includes four additional stages, they are beyond the scope of this book.

133

134

CONCLUSION

Today our industry finds itself at the brink of systemic transformation—a tentative state defined by Malcolm Gladwell as the "tipping point" (Gladwell 2006). School systems are overwhelmed by the sheer number of technology solutions that target various components of the education system but fail to address other, equally important and interdependent areas. Leaders, educators, and other stakeholders are increasingly frustrated by the rate of technological change—especially as districts engage in an ever-repeating cycle of acquiring and abandoning solutions after they fail to adequately meet the system's needs and bring about positive transformation. Parents and students are increasingly questioning the paradigm of the traditional school system, as technology continues to redefine their expectations and experiences in other segments of their lives. And across the country, school districts are continually grappling with the clash between technology and the traditional processes, policies, and mental models of K–12 education. As K–12 education faces significant uncertainty, the need for a more thoughtful and systematic approach to technology integration has never been more essential.

We work in an environment of unique obstacles and challenges—all of which have complicated our ability to move forward with the same relative ease as other industries. Yet despite these challenges, we are beginning to make exciting progress. Today, a handful of districts have made remarkable strides in their journey toward Digital Convergence, and they are now realizing the early fruits of their labor. For these districts, the modern learning environment is no longer a grand vision, but a realistic goal within reach. Their superintendents are leading the transition by setting the direction, fostering engagement, and creating alignment. Their instructional staff and stakeholders are redesigning pedagogical practices and assessment methods to enhance, rather than diminish, learning in a blended, personalized learning environment. Their curriculum writers, teachers, and other stakeholders are redesigning curriculum through a modern lens. Their educators and IT staff are developing processes and infrastructure to support an integrated network of digital resources. And their instructional coaches and other stakeholders are designing professional learning programs that offer the same personalized experience their students are now receiving.

These districts have demonstrated that the storm of technological change—no matter how turbulent or ominous—can be tempered through a systematic, coordinated process that unifies the efforts of stakeholders across the education system's core components.

Yet the journey is far from complete. We've explored the early and emerging progress of districts engaged in the first three stages of Digital Convergence, but the more remarkable and exciting work lies ahead. As districts journey into the last four stages of Digital Convergence, they begin to realize the extraordinary results that truly transform teaching and learning for the twenty-first century. Districts reaching these phases unlock new possibilities for students, teachers, and other stakeholders. In Stages 4 and 5, districts begin to realize significant benefits from their work to transition to modern learning environments. In Stages 6 and 7, districts achieve the full potential of technology to improve outcomes. In subsequent editions, I explore these stages in detail through the lens of the Digital Convergence Framework and offer practical methods for continuing your journey.

THE FUTURE OF CONVERGENCE

Let's conclude with a glimpse at what is possible, given our ongoing commitment to the work of Digital Convergence.

Think of your district. Now, imagine it with the following characteristics across the five drivers of Digital Convergence:

You're no longer overwhelmed by the rate of technological change. You understand the ever-changing landscape of technology and how it affects learning, which you regularly communicate to stakeholders to keep them informed and prepared.

Your district is better prepared to produce graduates who meet the needs of society than ever before. Your instructional model is continuously updated to reflect these needs—producing graduates who have the competencies to effectively compete on a global scale.

Your curriculum is dynamic and flexible to the extent that it's updated "just in time" using the digital tools and resources in your ecosystem.

Your ecosystem is fully integrated and interoperable. Supported by multiple vendors, your ecosystem integrates new technologies automatically as they're procured—ensuring users receive complete access and a seamless experience.

Your professional learning programs are always current and continuously updated to reflect ongoing enhancements to curriculum, technology, and instructional design and delivery. Your professional learning programs personalize learning for all teachers, staff, and other stakeholders and enhance the accessibility, consistency, and replicability of learning.

Your district remains continuously coordinated, aligned, and supported as it keeps pace with the accelerated rate of technological, global, and environmental change.

These are a few of the many possibilities of Digital Convergence—a reason I urge you to continue the worthy pursuit of the modern, personalized learning environment. The journey is often challenging, tumultuous, and ongoing, but it's well worth the reward.

APPENDIX

DIGITAL CONVERGENCE FRAMEWORK

─────────────── E M E R G I N G ───────────────

STAGE 1

Leadership

1. Message from the Top (MFTT) – The Superintendent has communicated the desire to leverage technology to transform teaching and learning and has invited all stakeholders to co-construct the vision of the modern learning environment
2. Cross-functional team has been formed and serves as the district's Digital Convergence Steering Committee
3. A Theory of Action has been developed for the transformation of teaching and learning through Digital Convergence
4. Stakeholders have been identified and engaged in activities around the Theory of Action and the construction of the vision of the modern learning environment

Instructional Models

5. Cross-functional team has been formed to explore new instructional models. One person has been designated as the owner
6. Cross-functional team begins conversations about a newly defined instructional model, including use of learner profiles, blended and personalized learning and a competency-based education system
7. Cross-functional team begins conversations about adopting a framework for assessing instructional rigor
8. Cross-functional team begins conversations about adopting a framework for twenty-first century skills

Modern Curriculum

9. The district is beginning to explore a common blended unit plan across all subjects, courses, and grade levels

Digital Ecosystems

10. Cross-functional team is formed to explore the district's digital ecosystem. One person is designated as the owner

11. District begins conversations about its digital ecosystem including its purpose, users, systems, subsystems, and functions, and how it will support and align to the district's instructional model

Professional Learning

12. Cross-functional team is formed to develop, deploy, and monitor the district's professional learning and growth as it relates to Digital Convergence. One person is designated as the owner

STAGE 2

Leadership

13. Message from the Top – The Superintendent has communicated to stakeholders the successful development of the vision of the modern learning environment

14. Modern Learning Environment Vision Deck has been developed and delivered to all stakeholders

15. District common language glossary of terms has been developed and published with a plan to maintain and update over time

16. A brand for the Digital Convergence has been defined

17. The work of Digital Convergence is aligned to your district's strategic plan

Instructional Models

18. District-wide instructional model defined

19. Agreed upon framework for assessing instructional rigor

20. Agreed upon framework for assessing twenty-first century skills

Modern Curriculum

21. The district has conducted an assessment of its digital content, including its purchased content and where teachers are accessing free content

22. A common blended unit plan that is aligned with the new instructional model has been developed by the district across all subjects, courses, and grade levels

23. Model digital/blended lessons have been developed, are aligned with the new instructional model, and are available inside the district's digital ecosystem

Digital Ecosystems

24. The district has defined the digital ecosystem's purpose and users

25. The district has defined the digital ecosystem's systems, subsystems, and their functions

26. The district has procured a learning management system as part of their digital ecosystem

27. The district extends the brand of Digital Convergence to its ecosystem, including a name for the ecosystem, stakeholder communication, and visuals to represent the conceptual design

28. The district has conducted an assessment of its instructional digital tools, including both purchased tools and high access free tool

Professional Learning

29. The district has identified a professional learning implementation model with the necessary resources to support its success

30. Coaches to support Digital Convergence have been identified consistent with the district's implementation model

31. A professional learning plan has been developed consistent with the district's implementation model and includes corresponding timelines

32. A critical mass of coaches of Digital Convergence is ready and prepared with the knowledge, materials, and time to

support the initial cohort launch

33. An initial group of teachers is selected and grouped in professional learning cohorts consistent with the district's implementation model

34. Coaches of Digital Convergence have kicked off their teacher cohorts with a face to face session to set expectations, build awareness of tools and resources, and generate excitement for the journey ahead

STAGE 3

Leadership

35. Message from the Top – The Superintendent has communicated to all stakeholders key wins in Digital Convergence during the first two stages and continues to update all stakeholders with next steps in the work

36. All school-based leaders have been trained on leading change: change management theory, 1st and 2nd order change

37. School-based plans have been created for "culture conversations"

38. School-based leaders have facilitated "culture conversations" around Digital Convergence and the need to transform teaching and learning

39. Plans to communicate the work of Digital Convergence (internally and externally) through various media outlets are continuous and on-going

40. Clearly defined metrics for each conversion and a formal review process have been established within the organization

Instructional Models

41. Additional key instructional staff have been identified and engaged in providing feedback around the newly defined instructional model

Modern Curriculum

42. Model blended units have been developed, are aligned to the new instructional model, and are available inside the

district's digital ecosystem

43. The district has identified gaps in digital content across all subjects, courses, and grade levels and has a plan to address the gaps

Digital Ecosystems

44. Regular cadence has been established for the Digital Eco-system Team while integration needs, progress monitoring, and milestones are continuously reviewed

45. A hierarchical rollout to stakeholder groups has been defined and a go-live date has been set first for internal testing, and then tiered access

Professional Learning

46. School-based leadership professional learning is in progress with clear evidence that the team continuously monitors effectiveness based upon a number of data points

47. Professional learning plans have been developed for new teacher induction and include a pathway for all new teachers to be fluent in Digital Convergence within the first 3 years of their employment

48. Coaches of Digital Convergence professional learning is in progress with clear evidence that the team continuously monitors effectiveness based upon a number of data points

49. Teacher cohort professional learning is in progress with clear evidence that the team continuously monitors effectiveness based upon a number of data points

50. A critical mass of school-based leadership has achieved literacy in change management practices

51. A critical mass of coaches of Digital Convergence has achieved literacy in the role of Architect

52. A critical mass of coaches of Digital Convergence has achieved fluency in the role of Architect

53. 10% of the district's teachers have achieved literacy in the role of Architect

54. 10% of the district's teachers have achieved fluency in the role of Architect
55. The district begins to talk about student outcome metrics going beyond quantitative state assessments

--------------------- GOOD ---------------------

STAGE 4

Leadership

56. MFTT – Messaging reflects a relentless pursuit of Digital Convergence excellence. Wins are celebrated during the first four stages while continuously focusing all stakeholders towards the realization of the desired vision
57. District leadership and school-based leadership participate in "problems of practice" inquiry (instructional rounds) based upon four critical questions: What is the teacher doing or saying? What are the students doing or saying? What is the instructional task? What is the role of technology in the lesson? These questions tie back to the district's newly defined instructional model
58. District leadership begins to align new instructional model with teacher evaluations

Instructional Models

59. Grade policy is updated to reflect competency-based system

Modern Curriculum

60. District communicates its desire to provide increased opportunities for students to leverage technology to create content and not just be passive consumers

Digital Ecosystems

61. All vendors that make up the district's digital ecosystem have contractually committed to the integration work/ standards or provided the district a timeline for additional development needs
62. Protocols have been established for regular testing (QA) of

145

information systems and user access to the ecosystem as a result of any unforeseen updates and/or bugs

Professional Learning

63. A critical mass of School-based leadership has achieved fluency in change management practices
64. A critical mass of coaches of Digital Convergence has achieved literacy in the roles of Manager, Facilitator, and Coach
65. 10% of the district's teachers have achieved literacy in the roles of Manager, Facilitator, and Coach
66. 10% of the district's teachers have achieved fluency in the roles of Manager, Facilitator, and Coach
67. 30% of the district's teachers have achieved literacy in the role of Architect
68. 30% of the district's teachers have achieved fluency in the role of Architect
69. The district begins to track and monitor student outcome metrics going beyond quantitative state assessments

STAGE 5

Leadership

70. MFTT – Messaging reflects the need for the organization to monitor, learn and adjust its Digital Convergence plans. Wins are continuously communicated while keeping the "eye on the prize"
71. School-based leaders use data to evaluate every teacher's proficiency with the new instructional model
72. School-based and teacher leaders move from awareness to action after "problems of practice" inquiry. School-based and individual teacher action plans are developed for school-wide improvement
73. Formal and informal celebrations and recognition are pervasive throughout the district culture

Instructional Models

74. Learner profiles have been researched, clearly defined, and part of the instructional model
75. A tool for assessing learner profiles is identified and procured
76. Some courses at the high school level are blended and teachers are empowered to make informed decisions regarding instructional time with students

Modern Curriculum

77. All blended units in all courses and subjects have opportunities for students to be creators of content through authentic problems as well as master core content knowledge

Digital Ecosystems

78. To build a comprehensive learner profile, the district's digital ecosystem team has reviewed and established all data that needs to be shared across the district's digital ecosystem. Further, user profiles (user access level) have been cross-referenced to ensure users only have access to the data sets that they need. Finally, the team has defined the cadence and frequency of data sharing for each set.

Professional Learning

79. A critical mass of coaches of Digital Convergence has achieved fluency in the roles of Manager, Facilitator, and Coach
80. 30% of the district's teachers have achieved literacy in the roles of Manager, Facilitator, and Coach
81. 30% of the district's teachers have achieved fluency in the roles of Manager, Facilitator, and Coach
82. 60% of the district's teachers have achieved literacy in the role of Architect
83. 60% of the district's teachers have achieved fluency in the role of Architect
84. The district continues to track and monitor student outcome metrics by expanding upon the metrics in Stage 4 and ensuring alignment to their Theory of Action, Vision, and Instructional Model

STAGE 6

Leadership

85. MFTT – Messaging reflects the district's stature as a model district based upon the hard work of all stakeholders. It reminds people of the focused work to get where they are, with a nudge to the future work ahead

86. The district's strategic plan is continuously examined with clear evidence of monitoring, updates, and adjustments documented

Instructional Models

87. Students progress through curriculum only after mastery

88. All students are assessed for their learner profile and are aware of "how they learn"

89. Students are grouped based upon characteristics in their learner profile rather than their age or grade level

90. Students have choice over the time, place, path, and pace of their learning

91. All courses at the high school level are blended and teachers are empowered to make informed decisions regarding instructional time with students

Modern Curriculum

92. The district's curriculum is continuously examined and monitored against the needs of society

Digital Ecosystems

93. A continuous feedback loop has been established between the District's Digital Ecosystem and all end user groups. Feedback is prioritized into an actionable development roadmap for the ecosystem

Professional Learning

94. Clear evidence exists that the professional learning team has fostered cross-collaboration opportunities among teachers that includes opportunities to observe and provide

peer-to-peer feedback and support within one's own school and across schools. There is a deep sense of reflection and practice with the key deliverable moving from fluency to mastery in Digital Convergence

95. A critical mass of coaches of Digital Convergence has achieved mastery in all roles for all modules

96. 60% of the district's teachers have achieved literacy in the roles of Manager, Facilitator, and Coach

97. 60% of the district's teachers have achieved fluency in the roles of Manager, Facilitator, and Coach

98. 90% of the district's teachers have achieved literacy in the role of Architect

99. 90% of the district's teachers have achieved fluency in the role of Architect

100. The district begins to schedule performance meetings at all levels of the organization to review data on the impact of Digital Convergence and student outcomes

STAGE 7

Leadership

101. MFTT – District leadership communicates with all stakeholders on a regular basis about the ever-changing landscape of technology and how it affects learning

102. The district's vision is updated to reflect the new needs of society

Instructional Models

103. The district's instructional model is continuously examined against the needs of society and best practices for learning. As technology adapts and changes the district refines their instructional model to meet these needs

Modern Curriculum

104. District curriculum is updated "just in time" by utilizing its technology tools and digital ecosystem

Digital Ecosystems

105. The district's digital ecosystem has become a multi-vendor, interconnected and interactive tool that meets the needs of a diverse group of stakeholders. As new technologies become available the ecosystem is nimble enough to integrate these tools within the structures of the ecosystem

Professional Learning

106. Professional learning team continuously monitors curriculum adjustments, technology upgrades/changes, and best practices for instructional design and delivery and has a systemic plan to update training content and modules on a continuous basis

107. The district has regularly scheduled performance meetings at all levels of the organization to review data on the impact of Digital Convergence and student outcomes

108. 90% of the district's teachers have achieved literacy in the roles of Manager, Facilitator, and Coach

109. 90% of the district's teachers have achieved fluency in the roles of Manager, Facilitator, and Coach

110. District defined student outcomes metric here

151

CITATIONS

Braun, William. 2002. "The System Archetypes." *University at Albany*. Accessed May 16. http://www.albany.edu/

Bridges, William. 2009. Managing Transitions: *Making the Most of Change*. Philadelphia: Da Capo Press. Kindle Edition.

Collins, Jim. 2001. *Good to Great: Why Some Companies Make the Leap...And Others Don't*. New York: HarperCollins. Kindle Edition.

Friedman, Thomas L. 2016. *Thank You for Being Late: An Optimist's Guide to Thriving in the Age of Accelerations*. New York: Farrar, Straus and Giroux. Kindle Edition.

Gladwell, Malcolm. 2006. *The Tipping Point: How Little Things Can Make a Big Difference*. New York: Little, Brown and Company.

Gray, Lucinda, Thomas, Nina, Lewis, Laurie. 2010. *Teachers' Use of Education Technology in U.S. Public Schools: 2009*. Washington DC: US Department of Education.

Greenhow, Christine, Robelia, Beth, Hughes, Joan E. 2016. "Learning, Teaching, and Scholarship in a Digital Age: Web 2.0 and Classroom Research: What Path Should We Take Now?" *EDUCATIONAL RESEARCHER* 38.4: 246-259.

Higgins, Steve, Beauchamp, Gary, Miller, Dave. 2007. "Reviewing the literature on interactive Whiteboards." *Learning, Media and Technology* 32.3: 213-225.

Hood, David. 2015. *The Rhetoric and The Reality: New Zealand
Schools and Schooling in the 21st Century*. Masterton, NZ:
Fraser Books.

Hull, Jim. 2010. "Cutting to the bone: How the economic crisis
affects schools." *Center for Public Education*. Accessed
November 4. http://www.centerforpubliceducation.org/
Main-Menu/Public-education/Cutting-to-the-bone-At-a-
glance/Cutting-to-the-bone-How-the-economic-crisis-affects-
schools.html

Kurzweil, Ray. 2000. *The Age of Spiritual Machines: When Computers
Exceed Human Intelligence*. New York: Penguin Publishing
Group. Kindle Edition.

National Center for Education Statistics. 2010. "Number and
internet access of instructional computers and rooms in
public schools, by selected characteristics: Selected years, 1995
through 2008." Accessed November 4. https://nces.ed.gov/
programs/digest/d10/tables/dt10_108.asp

Sinek, Simon. 2009. *Start with Why: How Great Leaders Inspire
Everyone to Take Action*. New York: Penguin Publishing Group.
Kindle Edition.

Wells, John, Lewis, Laurie. 2006. *Internet Access in U.S. Public
Schools and Classrooms: 1994-2005*. Washington DC:
US Department of Education.

ABOUT THE AUTHOR

 Shawn K. Smith is currently serving as President of Modern Teacher and is a national leader on issues surrounding digital education and pedagogy. He is compelled to preserve education's rich heritage and support America's teachers and leaders as they transition traditional classrooms into modern learning environments.

154 | He is an author, speaker, consultant, and rare book collector. He has one of the largest private collections of John Dewey's writings in the world. Formerly Shawn was a teacher, principal, and Chief of Schools for 15 years in school districts in Illinois and California. He has made appearances on both Discovery and Learning channels as well as various radio, web, and podcast programs. Shawn holds degrees from Carthage College in Kenosha, Wisconsin (bachelor's degree, elementary education), the California State University, San Bernardino (master's degree, middle school education), and the University of Southern California (doctorate degree, urban education policy and leadership).

DIGITAL CONVERGENCE ASSESSMENT

To learn where your school district stands in the journey toward Digital Convergence, take the Digital Convergence Assessment. This open-source assessment identifies your district's starting point and immediate action items to create a personalized, or modern, learning environment.

To access the assessment, visit
https://modernteacher.com/framework.

155

modern
teacher

Modern Teacher.
Transitioning traditional classrooms to modern
learning environments.

Through a proven framework and national network, Modern Teacher supports K-12 school districts implementing personalized and blended learning. We are an educational technology company with a research-based methodology for Digital Convergence in education and a technology-enabled solution to connect and support districts in leveraging today's tools across K-12 classrooms. We have assembled a network of like-minded professionals dedicated to supporting teachers in today's highly connected, digital world.

To learn more about Modern Teacher, visit:
www.modernteacher.com